CW00820466

Service Integration and Management (SIAM™) Foundation Body of Knowledge (BoK)

Second edition

Service Integration and Management (SIAM™) Foundation Body of Knowledge (BoK)

Second edition

CLAIRE AGUTTER ET AL.

IT Governance Publishing

Every possible effort has been made to ensure that the information contained in this book is accurate at the time of going to press, and the publisher and the author cannot accept responsibility for any errors or omissions, however caused. Any opinions expressed in this book are those of the author, not the publisher. Websites identified are for reference only, not endorsement, and any website visits are at the reader's own risk. No responsibility for loss or damage occasioned to any person acting, or refraining from action, as a result of the material in this publication can be accepted by the publisher or the author.

Apart from any fair dealing for the purposes of research or private study, or criticism or review, as permitted under the Copyright, Designs and Patents Act 1988, this publication may only be reproduced, stored or transmitted, in any form, or by any means, with the prior permission in writing of the publisher or, in the case of reprographic reproduction, in accordance with the terms of licences issued by the Copyright Licensing Agency. Enquiries concerning reproduction outside those terms should be sent to the publisher at the following address:

IT Governance Publishing Ltd
Unit 3, Clive Court
Bartholomew's Walk
Cambridgeshire Business Park
Ely, Cambridgeshire
CB7 4EA
United Kingdom
www.itgovernancepublishing.co.uk

© Claire Agutter 2021

The author has asserted the rights of the author under the Copyright, Designs and Patents Act, 1988, to be identified as the author of this work.

First edition published in 2017 by Van Haren Publishing.

Second edition published in the United Kingdom in 2021 by IT Governance Publishing

ISBN 978-1-78778-310-2

SIAM™ is a Registered Trademark of EXIN.

COBIT® is a Registered Trademark of the Information Systems Audit and Control Association and the IT Governance Institute.

ITIL®, PRINCE2® and M_o_R® are Registered Trademarks of AXELOS Limited.

ISO® is a Registered Trademark of the International Organization for Standardization.

OBASHI is a Licenced Trademark of OBASHI Ltd.

Cynefin is a Trademark of Cognitive Edge Ptd Ltd.

ADKAR® is a Registered Trademark of Prosci Inc.

SFIA® is a Registered Trademark of the SFIA Foundation Limited.

CMMI® is a Registered Trademark owned by Carnegie Mellon University.

TOGAF® is a Registered Trademark of The Open Group.

PMI® and PMBOK® are Registered Trademarks of the Project Management Institute, Inc.

FOREWORD

The idea of creating content related to SIAM first came to me in 2016. The service management world was developing rapidly and I could see that SIAM was being applied in more and more organizations to help manage complex sourcing environments, particularly for IT services. It was surprising, however, that there was little detailed SIAM content available to support practitioners using the methodology.

The idea of the SIAM Body of Knowledge (BoK) was born and I set up the SIAM Architect Group, involving volunteers from all around the world and from different types and sizes of organization. We formed a strong team and created the Foundation BoK. Our aim was to offer standard SIAM terms, guidance and content that anyone in the ecosystem could use.

Since its launch, the SIAM Foundation BoK has been downloaded more than 10,000 times. Hundreds of people around the world have taken SIAM training and passed the SIAM Foundation exam. In 2017, the architect team expanded and we developed the SIAM Professional BoK, led by Chief Architects Michelle Major-Goldsmith and Simon Dorst, providing more detailed practical guidance.

Scopism continues to be active in the SIAM sector, hosting a SIAM-focused conference and publishing the global SIAM survey. The interest we see, and the survey results, show that SIAM is still growing, with some geographies more mature than others. Digital transformation is driving the adoption of SIAM as a sourcing model, as organizations embed technology in the heart of their business strategy.

The second edition of the SIAM Foundation BoK reflects changes in the market, but the underlying principles remain true. I am very grateful for the generosity of the SIAM community that has allowed us to create these valuable publications.

Claire Agutter

About Claire Agutter

Claire Agutter is a service management trainer, consultant and author, and director of ITSM Zone and Scopism. In 2018 she was recognized as an HDI Top 25 Thought Leader and was part of the team that won itSMF UK's Thought Leadership award for the SIAM Foundation BoK. Claire is the host of the popular ITSM Crowd hangouts and is Chief Architect for VeriSM™.

For more information about Claire's other publications, visit:
www.itgovernancepublishing.co.uk/author/claire-agutter.

CONTENTS

ABOUT THIS BOOK

Authors and contributors

Scopism would like to thank the following people and organizations for their contributions to this book:

Atos

- Trisha Booth
- Chris Bullivant
- Harry Burnett
- Charlotte Parnham

Independents

- Rajiv Dua
- Kevin Holland
- Caroline Trill
- Duncan Watkins

ISG

- Simon Durbin
- Dean Hughes
- Andrea Kis

ITSM Value

- David Baughan
- Damian Bowen

Kinetic IT

- Simon Dorst
- Michelle Major-Goldsmith

Scopism

- Claire Agutter

Sopra Steria

- Nicola Boland-Hill
- Alison Cartlidge
- Anna Leyland
- Susan North

Syniad IT

- Steve Morgan

TCS

- James Finister

Second edition

The following volunteers contributed to the second edition of this book:

- Alison Cartlidge, Sopra Steria
- Angelo Leisinger, CLAVIS klw AG
- Anna Leyland, Sopra Steria
- Biju Pillai, Capgemini
- Claire Agutter, Scopism
- Damian Bowen, acrinax
- Jacob Andersen, Independent
- Kevin Holland, Independent
- Liz Gallacher, Helix SMS Ltd
- Michelle Major-Goldsmith, Kinetic IT
- Morten Bukh Dreier, Valcon

- Reni Friis, Valcon
- Sachin Bhatnagar, South32
- Simon Dorst, Kinetic IT

The purpose of *Service Integration and Management (SIAM™) Foundation Body of Knowledge (BoK), Second edition*

This book introduces service integration and management (SIAM). Its contents are the source material for the EXIN SIAM™ Foundation certification.[1]

---

[1] *www.exin.com/certifications/exin-siamtm-foundation-exam*.

CHAPTER 1: INTRODUCTION TO SERVICE INTEGRATION AND MANAGEMENT (SIAM)

1.1 What is SIAM?

Service integration and management (SIAM) is a management methodology that can be applied in an environment that includes services sourced from a number of service providers.

SIAM has a different level of focus to traditional multi-sourced ecosystems with one customer and multiple suppliers. It provides governance, management, integration, assurance and coordination to ensure that the customer organization gets maximum value from its service providers.

SIAM governance operates at three levels in the ecosystem:

- Strategic
- Tactical
- Operational

SIAM is an evolution of how to apply a framework for integrated service management across multiple service providers. It has developed as organizations have moved away from outsourced contracts with a single supplier to an environment with multiple service providers. SIAM has evolved from the challenges associated with these more complex operating models.

SIAM supports cross-functional, cross-process and cross-provider integration. It creates an environment where all parties:

- Know their role, responsibilities and context in the ecosystem
- Are empowered to deliver
- Are held accountable for the outcomes they are required to deliver

SIAM introduces the concept of a service integrator, which is a single, logical entity held accountable for the end-to-end delivery of services and the business value that the customer receives.

> **Terminology**
>
> SIAM is the generally accepted acronym for service integration and management.
>
> Other acronyms that are in use are:
>
> - MSI (Multi-sourcing Integration)
> - SMI (Service Management Integration)
> - SI (Service Integration)
> - SMAI (Service Management and Integration)
> - SI&M (Service Integration & Management)

SIAM can be applied to different sizes and types of organization, and to different industry sectors. Customers that only require a single service provider are unlikely to get the full value from SIAM.

SIAM can be applied to environments that include external service providers only, internal service providers only, or a combination of internal and external service providers. The effectiveness of SIAM and the value it delivers will increase as the number of service providers and the number of interactions between services increase.

Some organizational cultures are more able to adapt to SIAM than others. Effective SIAM requires control to be balanced with trust, devolution of responsibilities, openness, and collaboration across all parties. A transition to SIAM is likely to require significant changes in attitude, behavior, and culture in ecosystems that previously relied on command-and-control structures for effective service delivery.

The SIAM methodology encompasses:

- Practices
- Processes
- Functions
- Roles
- Structural elements

The customer organization will transition to a SIAM model developed from these elements.

1.1.1 The SIAM ecosystem

There are three layers in a SIAM ecosystem:

1. Customer organization (including retained capabilities)
2. Service integrator
3. Service provider(s)

Each layer has a role as part of effective end-to-end management of services and the delivery of maximum value. Each layer should have sufficient capability and maturity to fulfil its role.

1.1.1.1 Customer organization

The customer organization is the end client that is making the transition to SIAM as part of its operating model. It commissions the SIAM ecosystem.

Customer organizations typically contain business units such as human resources, finance, sales and their own internal IT function. They also have their own customers that use their products and services.

Figure 1 shows the layers of the SIAM ecosystem, and the consumers of services from the customer organization.

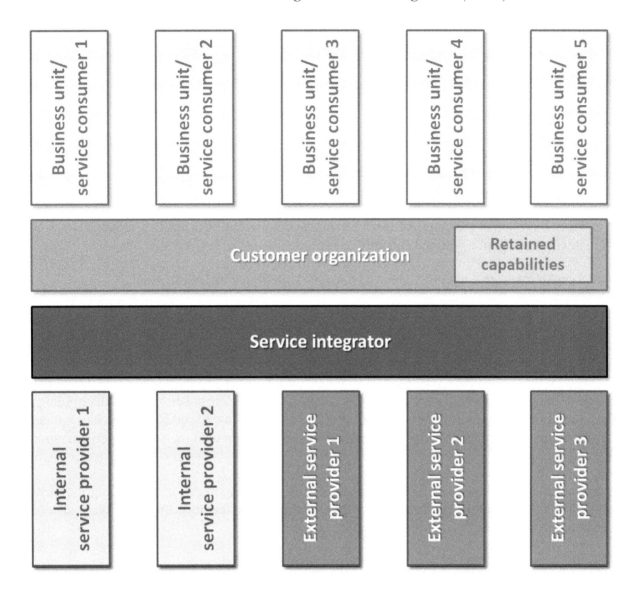

Figure 1: The SIAM layers, including consumers of services from the customer organization

In this book, we use the terms 'customer organization' and 'customer' to mean the commissioning organization.

The customer organization will own the contractual relationships with external service providers, and with any external service integrator.

1.1.1.2 Retained capabilities

The customer organization will include some retained capabilities. The retained capabilities are the functions that are responsible for strategic, architectural, business engagement and corporate governance activities.

These business-differentiating functions typically remain under the direct control and ownership of the customer organization. Retained capabilities also include any accountabilities and responsibilities that must remain with the customer for legislative or regulatory reasons.

Examples of possible retained capabilities are:

- Enterprise architecture
- Policy and standards management
- Procurement
- Contract management
- Demand management
- Financial and commercial management
- Service portfolio management
- Corporate risk management
- Governance of the service integrator; based on achievement of business outcomes

The service integrator is independent from the retained capabilities, even if it is internally sourced. Service integration is not a retained capability.

Retained capabilities are sometimes referred to as the 'intelligent client function'.

1.1.1.3 Service integrator

The service integrator layer of the SIAM ecosystem is where end-to-end service governance, management, integration, assurance and coordination is performed.

The service integrator layer focuses on implementing an effective cross-service provider organization, making sure that all service providers are contributing to the end-to-end service. It provides operational governance over the service providers and has a direct relationship with the customer organization and the service providers.

The service integrator layer can be provided by one or more organizations, including the customer organization. If the service integrator layer is provided by more than one organization, it should still be considered a single logical service integrator.

The service integrator can include one team of people or multiple teams.

1.1.1.4 Service provider

Within a SIAM ecosystem, there are multiple service providers. Each service provider is responsible for the delivery of one or more services, or service elements, to the customer. It is also responsible for managing the products and technology used to deliver its contracted or agreed services and operating its own processes.

Service providers within a SIAM ecosystem are sometimes referred to as 'towers'. This term implies isolation and a monolithic approach, so the term 'service provider' is used as standard in this book.

Service providers can be part of the customer organization or external to it:

- An external service provider is an organization that is not part of the customer organization. Its performance is typically managed using service level agreements and a contract with the customer organization
- An internal service provider is a team or department that is part of the customer organization. Its performance is typically managed using internal agreements and targets

Examples of services provided by service providers in a SIAM model include:

- Desktop services/end-user computing
- Data center
- Hosting
- Security
- Network/LAN/WAN
- Cloud services
- Printing services
- Voice and video (VVI)
- Application development, support and maintenance
- Managed services

If the customer retains its own internal IT capability, this should be treated as an internal service provider, governed by the service integrator.

Service provider categories

It can be helpful to categorize service providers in a SIAM ecosystem to help define their importance to the customer organization and the approach to governing and assuring their services.

There are three common categories of service provider in a SIAM ecosystem:

- Strategic service provider
- Tactical service provider
- Commodity service provider

SIAM is applied to all three categories, but the nature of the relationship and the amount of management required will be different.

Figure 2 shows a high-level view of the SIAM layers.

Figure 2: The SIAM layers

The focus, activities and responsibilities of each layer are different. **Figure 3** provides an illustration.

Figure 3: Focus of the SIAM layers

1.1.2 SIAM practices

> **Practice:** *"the actual application or use of an idea, belief, or method, as opposed to theories relating to it."*[2]

SIAM includes specific practices that differentiate it from other management frameworks. These practices support governance, management, integration, assurance and coordination across the layers.

Examples of practices are described in **section 6**.

- **People practices:** managing cross-functional teams
- **Process practices:** integrating processes across service providers
- **Measurement practices:** reporting on end-to-end services
- **Technology practices:** creating a tooling strategy

SIAM also draws on other areas of IT and management 'best practice' – see **section 4**.

---

[2] *www.lexico.com/definition/practice*.

1.1.3 SIAM and processes

> **Process:** a documented, repeatable approach to carrying out a series of tasks or activities.

SIAM itself is not a process; it draws on and uses other management processes.

Most management approaches expect processes to be executed within one organization. In SIAM, these processes may also be executed:

- Across organizations in the same SIAM layer
- Across organizations in different SIAM layers

Many of the processes used within a SIAM ecosystem are familiar ones like change management and business relationship management. Within a SIAM model, however, these processes require adaptation to support integration and coordination between the different parties. They also require alignment with the SIAM practices.

Although this is not an exhaustive list, processes used within a SIAM ecosystem can include:

- Audit and control
- Business relationship management
- Change management
- Release management
- Commercial/contract management
- Continual improvement
- Event management
- Financial management
- Incident management
- Request fulfilment
- Service catalog management
- Information security management
- Knowledge management
- Monitoring, measuring, and reporting
- Problem management
- Project management
- Software asset and configuration management
- Service level management
- Service portfolio management
- Supplier management
- Toolset and information management
- Capacity and availability management
- Service continuity management
- Service introduction, retirement, and replacement

These processes need to be allocated to the appropriate layers in the SIAM model. This allocation may be different for each implementation of SIAM.

Some processes will span multiple layers. For example, the customer organization and the service integrator can both carry out elements of supplier management; the service integrator and service providers will each have responsibilities in the end-to-end change management process.

1.1.4 SIAM functions

> **Function:** *"an organizational entity, typically characterized by a special area of knowledge or experience."*[3]

Each organization in the SIAM ecosystem will determine its own organizational structure. This structure will include functions that execute specific processes and practices.

The service integration layer in the SIAM ecosystem has specific functions. These are where the service integrator carries out the activities for governance, management, assurance, integration and coordination.

While these functions may seem similar at a high level to those from other management methodologies, the activities can be different as they primarily focus on coordination and integration as opposed to operational activities.

The precise functions will vary for different implementations of SIAM, as they are dependent on the definition of roles and responsibilities across the ecosystem, and the detail of the SIAM model that has been adopted.

1.1.5 SIAM roles

Roles and responsibilities need to be defined, established, monitored and improved within a SIAM ecosystem.

This includes the roles and responsibilities of each:

- Layer
- Organization
- Function
- Structural element

High-level policies for roles and responsibilities are defined during the Discovery & Strategy stage of the SIAM roadmap. More detail is added during the Plan & Build stage.

Roles and responsibilities are allocated to relevant parties during the Implement stage. They are then monitored during Run & Improve and amended as required.

---

[3] ITIL Functions, Wikipedia: *https://wiki.en.it-processmaps.com/index.php/ITIL_Functions*.

1.1.6 SIAM structural elements

Within SIAM, 'structural elements' are organizational entities that have specific responsibilities and work across multiple organizations and layers in the SIAM ecosystem.

These structural elements link the functions with the practices, processes, and roles of SIAM.

The role of the structural elements includes:

- Governance
- Developing and maintaining policies
- Developing and maintaining data and information standards
- Reviewing and improving end-to-end service performance
- Reviewing and improving capability and maturity
- Identifying, encouraging and driving continual service improvements and innovation
- Resolving shared issues and conflicts
- Delivering specific projects
- Integrating, aggregating and consolidating data to form an end-to-end view
- Recognizing and rewarding success

Structural elements include representatives from the service integrator, service providers and, where required, the customer.

Using structural elements helps to establish relationships between the different parties. This encourages communication and collaboration, as attendees work together to achieve shared goals.

The use of structural elements differentiates SIAM from other methodologies and helps to facilitate the desired outcomes from SIAM.

There are three types of structural elements:

- Boards
- Process forums
- Working groups

1.1.6.1 Boards

Boards perform governance in the SIAM ecosystem.

They are formal decision-making bodies, and are accountable for the decisions that they take. Boards will convene regularly, for as long as the SIAM model is in place.

In SIAM, governance activities are carried out by boards acting at strategic, tactical and operational levels. Examples are:

- **Strategic:** approval of funding, contractual and commercial agreements, and strategy
- **Tactical:** approval of policies
- **Operational:** approval of changes to services and processes

1.1.6.2 Process forums

Process forums are aligned to specific processes or practices. Their members work together on proactive development, innovations, and improvements.

Forums will convene regularly, for as long as the SIAM model is in place. Their responsibilities include:

- Developing and sharing common working practices
- Developing data and information standards
- Continual improvement
- Innovation

For example, a problem management process forum can be established with problem management peers from each service provider and the service integrator. They can jointly develop a set of key performance indicators for the problem management process.

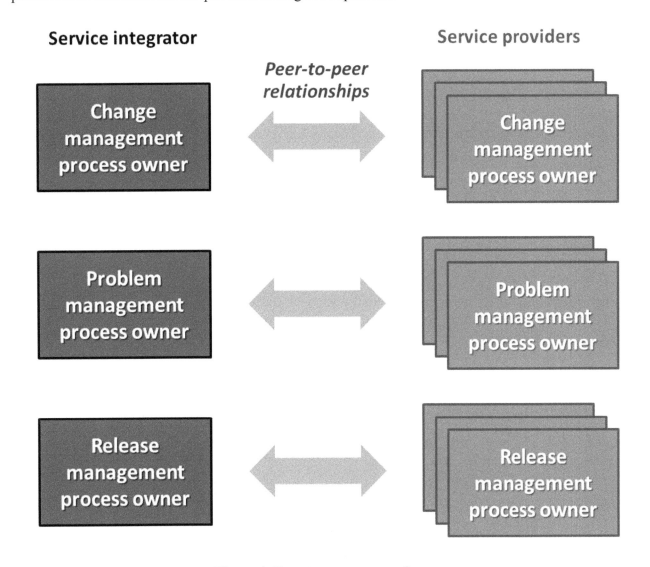

Figure 4: Peer-to-peer process forums

The scope of a process forum can be for a single process or for a group of related processes. For example, a single process forum could be established for the related processes of incident management and request management.

There is no requirement to create an individual process forum for every process. Where the scope overlaps, a single forum may address multiple processes. The value of the process forums will diminish if their remits overlap and work is duplicated, or if they are perceived as an unnecessary overhead.

1.1.6.3 Working groups

Working groups are convened to address specific issues or projects. They are typically formed on a reactive ad hoc or fixed-term basis. They can include staff from different organizations and different specialized areas.

For example: an ad hoc working group could be established with members from several service providers to investigate an intermittent issue with the performance of an integrated service. This could include specialists from capacity management, IT operations, development, problem management and availability management. Alternatively, a fixed-term working group could be established to manage the delivery of an integrated release. The members would be from all layers and from multiple processes and functions.

Process forums and working groups often involve the same people, so can be combined into the same meeting if appropriate. In these combined meetings, it is important to ensure that there is a focus on proactive as well as reactive activities.

1.1.7 SIAM models

Each organization will develop its own SIAM model, based on the layers in the SIAM ecosystem. The SIAM model that an organization adopts will be influenced by several factors:

- The services that are in scope
- The required outcomes
- The use of proprietary models by externally sourced service integrators

Because of this, there is no single 'perfect' SIAM model. No model is 'better' than any other, although some may be more suitable to particular implementations than others.

Different organizations adapt models to meet their own needs. All models share common characteristics that are aligned to the methodology described in this BoK.

Figure 5 shows a high-level SIAM model, including the relationships between SIAM layers practices, processes, functions, and structural elements.

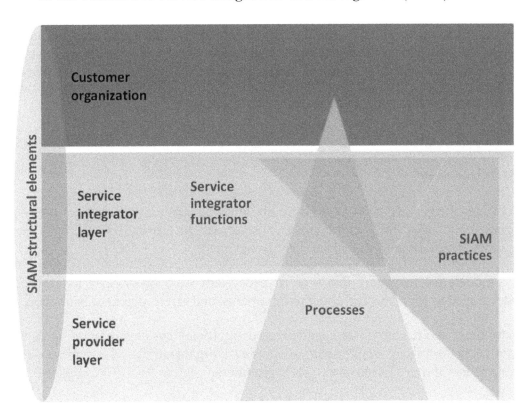

Figure 5: A high-level SIAM model

1.1.8 SIAM contractual and sourcing considerations

Within the SIAM model, the customer owns the contractual relationship with external service providers and any external service integrator.

The service integrator is empowered to act on behalf of the customer, exercising the parts of the contract related to the delivery of the services by the service providers.

The contracts between the service providers and the customer organization must make it clear that the service integrator is the agent of the customer, whether that service integrator is internally sourced or externally sourced.

To provide flexibility to support future business and technology strategies, where possible, the contracts should support changes to services and ways of working.

In many existing customer and provider relationships, standard contracts have limited the ability to transition to SIAM. For SIAM to be effective, the customer organization needs to select the right service providers and have suitable contracts in place.

SIAM contracts are typically shorter and more flexible than traditional IT outsourcing contracts. Targets within the contracts should encourage service providers to work together, including contributing to service improvements and innovation.

In a SIAM environment, the best outcomes are realized when the customer, service integrator, and service providers all work cooperatively to achieve common goals. Wherever possible, contracts should facilitate this, by being fair to all parties and by applying the terms in a transparent and impartial way.

Trust-based supplier management is more likely to achieve the necessary collaborative outcomes, rather than just relying on strict adherence through the terms of the contract. To establish this trust and fairness, it is necessary to consider the management practices and ways of working needed within the SIAM ecosystem. This is discussed in more detail in the *Service Integration and Management (SIAM™) Professional Body of Knowledge (BoK), Second edition.*[4]

1.2 The history of SIAM

1.2.1 SIAM as a concept

Organizations have been using services delivered by multiple service providers for many years. They have recognized the need for service integration across service providers, and used different approaches to try to achieve end-to-end service management.

Historically, models for managing this type of ecosystem were proprietary to very large service providers, developed to meet specific client requirements, and rarely shared outside those providers.

In most cases, these service providers also delivered significant systems integration capabilities, but with no clear separation from service integration. These organizations were typically referred to as Systems Integrators (SIs) or IT Outsource (ITO) providers.

1.2.2 The emergence of the term 'SIAM'

The term 'service integration and management', and the concept of SIAM as a management methodology originated in about 2005 from within the UK public sector, which was also the source of other best-practice methodologies such as ITIL®.

The methodology was initially designed for the Department for Work and Pensions to obtain better value for money from services delivered by multiple service providers, and specifically to separate service integration capabilities from systems integration and IT service provision.

This new approach reduced the duplication of activities in the service providers, and introduced the concept of a 'service integrator'. This new service integration capability provided governance and coordination to encourage service providers to work together to drive down costs and improve service quality.

SIAM was viewed as a methodology, not a function. Within the methodology, a service integrator provided a set of service integration capabilities.

The SIAM methodology that was emerging facilitated collaboration between the various service providers, and management of interfaces between them. The service integrator was 'one step above' the service provider layer.

Processes were used in the SIAM ecosystem to define activities, inputs, outputs, controls, and measurements. The methodology allowed individual service providers to act autonomously and define

---

[4] For more information, visit: *www.itgovernancepublishing.co.uk/product/service-integration-and-management-siam-professional-body-of-knowledge-bok-second-edition*.

the specific mechanisms that enabled those activities. These were then audited and assured by the service integrator.

Figure 6 shows a simple view of the SIAM model.

Figure 6: A simple view of a SIAM ecosystem

1.2.3 Growth and adoption of SIAM within the UK government

In 2010, the UK government published a new information and communications technology (ICT) strategy. This included moving away from large prime supplier contracts to a more flexible approach using multiple service providers and cloud-based solutions.

A paper was published in support of this strategy that set out a new approach for service management governance and organization. The proposal was to appoint an appropriate service management framework to coordinate multiple services, providers and consumers in a secure and seamless lifecycle of service delivery and improvement.

This accelerated the development and awareness of SIAM both in the UK public sector and elsewhere. This acceleration led to the publication in 2012 of the UK government 'Cross Government Strategic SIAM Reference Set'. This was developed from experience and expertise in SIAM from the Department for Work and Pensions, Ministry of Justice, NHS Connecting for Health and Government Procurement Service. **Figure 7** shows the SIAM Enterprise Model from this reference set.

The aim of the reference set was to enable transformation in UK public-sector organizations to a disaggregated, multi-sourced, multi-service environment.

The reference set described a wide range of SIAM capabilities and a suggested enterprise model, but encouraged adaptation to suit local requirements.

This was the first widely available description of SIAM. Its publication rapidly increased the awareness, development and discussion of SIAM worldwide.

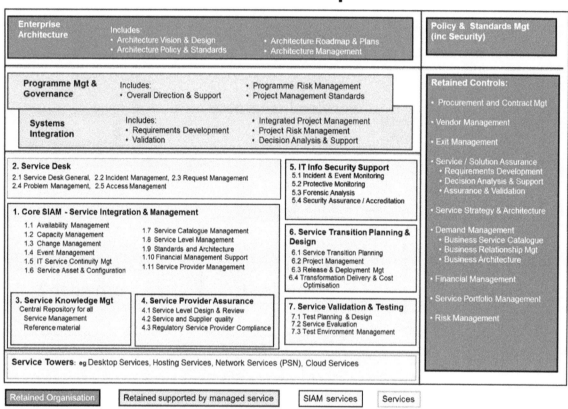

Figure 7: SIAM Enterprise Model from Service Integration & Management (SIAM) Framework Cross Government Reference Set, October 2012

The contemporary UK Government Service Design Manual advised that:

"The level of service integration will differ depending on the complexity of the business services and/or customers that are being supported, and the complexity of the services that are being delivered to those businesses. As the services and businesses become more critical or complex, the level of service integration becomes deeper.

The design of the service integration function will differ by department. It may be completely operated in-house. Or it might consist of a thin in-house capability ultimately responsible for the integrated end to end operation and management of quality IT services, underpinned by outsourced integration services for specific elements – for example performance monitoring, service desk, or

> *service level reporting. Particularly for smaller departments and simple services, care needs to be taken not to over-engineer the service integration approach – effective use of commodity standards-*
>
> *based IT should mean that integration and support requirements are much less onerous than managing a locked-down bespoke system.*"[5]

1.2.4 SIAM history

Approaches to SIAM and its adoption have increased significantly in the past ten years and advanced since the first iteration of this book in 2016. This has been driven by strategic factors, including:

- Increased complexity of sourcing models
- A worldwide need to improve value
- A desire to remove reliance on single suppliers
- The need for effective controls
- A desire for the ability and flexibility to use 'best of breed' service providers and services, including the use of commodity cloud-based services

The development and adoption of SIAM has been accompanied by an increase in the number of publications on SIAM and the number of commercial organizations offering service integration capabilities, many of which have their own SIAM model.

> *"Against a backdrop of increased business and IT complexity, the IT service provider is faced with a challenge to deliver more with less. Customers demand IT cost transparency and demonstrated value. Additionally, multi-sourced service delivery is the new reality for many. Both customers and users are demanding innovative technology solutions and access to each providers' specialisms, but do not necessarily want to be presented with the issues that controlling the complex web of multiple providers brings.*
>
> *The multi-provider delivery models evident in many modern enterprises have created an interest in the benefits SIAM can bring. More and more customers are calling for better defined and more cohesive control structures that will allow the management of multiple service providers in a consistent and efficient way. They demand performance across a portfolio of services that meets the needs of the users and can be flexed as the needs change.*"[6]

While SIAM itself may not be new, what is new is the recognition that SIAM is essential to support the delivery of value in multi-supplier ecosystems. There is evidence that this recognition is growing through the increased instances of:

- The incorporation of non-IT service providers into a SIAM ecosystem (sometimes referred to as 'enterprise SIAM')
- Internal service provider teams falling under the direction of a service integrator

---

[5] *www.gov.uk/service-manual*.

[6] "Who is the King of SIAM?" White Paper by Simon Dorst, Michelle Major-Goldsmith and Steve Robinson. Copyright © AXELOS 2015. All rights reserved.

1.3 The purpose of SIAM

"Effective SIAM seeks to combine the benefits of best-of-breed based multi-sourcing of services with the simplicity of single sourcing, minimizing the risks inherent in multi-sourced approaches and masking the supply chain complexity from the consumers of the services. SIAM is therefore appropriate for businesses that are moving to or already have a multi-sourced environment. The benefits of a well-designed, planned and executed SIAM model can be realized by businesses that use multiple external suppliers, a mix of internal and external suppliers, or several internal suppliers. SIAM is therefore appropriate for most of today's businesses."[7]

SIAM can, at first glance, seem to be simply an adaptation of commonly understood service management approaches such as ITIL, COBIT®, the Open Systems Interconnection (OSI) model or the Microsoft Operations Framework (MOF). Where SIAM differs is that it acknowledges and focuses on the specific challenges associated with multi-sourced service delivery models.

The service integrator provides the customer with a single point of accountability and control for the integrated delivery of services. This is achieved through the definition and application of controls within a robust governance methodology that also provides the necessary coordination between the service providers within the SIAM ecosystem. The service integrator also drives collaboration and improvement across the service providers, acting on behalf of the customer.

The service integrator takes ownership of these activities on behalf of the customer, allowing the customer organization to focus on the activities necessary for its business, rather than focusing on service providers and technology.

The service integrator manages the complexities of dealing with multiple service providers, allowing the customer to benefit from its specialisms and capabilities without incurring any additional management burden.

The application of the SIAM methodology creates an ecosystem where all parties involved in the delivery of the services are clear about their roles and responsibilities and are empowered to deliver within those boundaries.

SIAM also provides an understanding of the necessary interactions between the services and the service providers, and the techniques to manage those interactions effectively. This facilitates the coordination of delivery, integration and interoperability.

The service integrator provides assurance of the performance of individual service providers and over the end-to-end service, ensuring that the expected outcomes are delivered to the customer.

SIAM enables the flexibility and innovation necessary to support the pace of change demanded by today's fast-moving organizations.

---

[7] "An Example ITIL®-based Model for Effective Service Integration and Management" White Paper by Kevin Holland. Copyright © AXELOS 2015. All rights reserved.

1.4 The scope of SIAM

The scope of SIAM will vary from organization to organization. For the customer organization to derive any benefit from a transition to a SIAM model, the service(s) that are in scope must be defined.

This service definition makes it clear what is being governed, assured, integrated, coordinated and managed by the service integrator.

For each service within the scope of SIAM, the following areas need to be defined:

- Service outcomes, value, and objectives
- The service provider(s)
- The service consumer(s)
- The service characteristics, including service levels
- The service boundaries
- Dependencies with other services
- Technical interactions with other services
- Data and information interactions with other services

A service model should be created that shows the hierarchy of services. This hierarchy must clearly identify:

- Services that are directly consumed by the customer organization
- Underpinning services and dependencies

Figure 8 shows an example of a service model showing the service hierarchies.

The model shows how business needs in the customer organization are met by service provider services (lettered), and how in turn they are dependent on one or more supporting services (numbered), which may be delivered by an alternative provider.

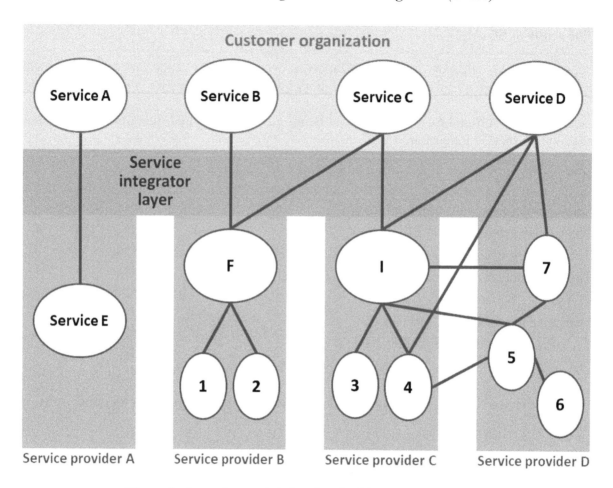

Figure 8: A service model showing the hierarchy of services

1.4.1 Types of service

SIAM can be applied to both IT services and technologies and non-IT services. Historically, it has mainly been adopted for IT services.

SIAM can be applied to managed services and cloud services, as well as to more traditional IT services, such as hosting or end-user computing.

Different organizations will have different types of services within the scope of their SIAM model. Some models may only include services that were previously provided by internal IT, as part of a strategy to outsource these services to external organizations.

Others may include a wide range of externally provided services and retain their internal IT department as an internal service provider. The customer organization will determine the scope in line with its strategy and requirements.

Examples of IT services include:

- Office productivity applications
- Customer relationship management systems
- Networks
- Bespoke customer applications

Examples of non-IT services that can be within the scope of SIAM are business processes such as sales order management, payroll processing, and consumer help desks.

Cloud services

SIAM can be applied to commodity services provided from the cloud. These include:

- Software as a Service (SaaS)
- Platform as a Service (PaaS)
- Infrastructure as a Service (IaaS)

Service providers for cloud services use the same delivery models for all of their customers. It is therefore unlikely that they will adapt their ways of working to align with a customer's specific SIAM requirements or accept governance from the service integrator.

If this is recognized and the service integrator can adapt to its approach while still delivering customer outcomes, SIAM can still be effective for these services.

1.5 SIAM and the business strategy

1.5.1 Why change?

Without effective service integration, many of the benefits anticipated from services delivered by multiple service providers can remain unrealized.

Transforming an organization to a SIAM model ensures that critical artefacts are developed as part of the SIAM roadmap. These will include:

- A clear design for how the overall end-to-end service will operate and integrate
- A standard governance approach
- A definition of accountability for the integrated service
- An end-to-end performance management and reporting framework
- Coordination between service providers
- Integration between the processes of different service providers
- A definition of roles and responsibilities
- A definition of ownership and coordination for incidents and problems that involve multiple suppliers

Organizations must be clear about why they want to adopt SIAM. Transitioning to a SIAM-based model is not an easy task. It will require investment and changes for all involved parties. The changes will affect areas including:

- Attitude, behavior, and culture
- Processes and procedures
- Capabilities
- Organizational structures
- Resources
- Knowledge

- Tools
- Contracts

Senior-level sponsorship and management commitment will be essential. Without management commitment, the transformation to a SIAM model is unlikely to succeed.

There are organizations for which SIAM is not appropriate. Before any organization embarks on a transition to SIAM, it must fully understand SIAM and the benefits it could derive. This will enable it to make a value-based judgement.

The organization can get this understanding in one of three ways, or in combination:

- Educate and train the staff who are leading on SIAM discovery and strategy in the SIAM methodology
- Seek help from outside the organization, either from similar organizations or from organizations experienced in SIAM adoption
- Recruit staff who have the required understanding and experience

1.5.2 Drivers for SIAM

In this context, a driver is defined as *"something that creates and fuels activity, or gives force and impetus"*.[8]

These drivers are the triggers that create an organization's desire to move to a SIAM model. Understanding the drivers for SIAM will help an organization to gain clarity of purpose.

The drivers will be used to create a business case for the transition to SIAM. They will also help the organization to maintain focus throughout the SIAM roadmap.

The challenges of delivery in a multi-service provider ecosystem

Service providers play a crucial role in helping a customer deliver its business outcomes. Poorly delivered services directly affect the customer's outcomes, and the service it can offer to its own customers.

This is true whether the services are delivered by one service provider or multiple service providers. However, the challenges of successful delivery are greater when there are multiple service providers, owing to increases in complexity and the interactions that need to take place between service providers.

Consider these scenarios that illustrate how poor service provision can have wider consequences:

---

[8] *www.collinsdictionary.com/dictionary/english/driver*.

- A hospital has booked in a patient to have an extensive medical scan. The medical machinery has stopped working and the cause of failure is unknown. The patient's appointment must be rescheduled. Will the delay to this appointment have a negative impact on the patient's health?
- A motoring organization cannot dispatch a patrol officer to assist a lone female motorist and her small child on a busy freeway because its command-and-control systems are unavailable owing to a failed system change. The organization does not know which patrol officers are available or where they are. To how much risk is the woman and her child exposed, and for how long?
- An online retailer is unable to cope with the increase in transactions before the holiday season. This makes its retail platform slow down, unnecessarily reject payments and at times show as unavailable. Will customers accept this or buy their goods and services elsewhere?

A hastily implemented, partially tested update to a travel agent's booking system has caused the personal information of its customers (including credit card details) to be hacked. The press has found out and is publishing worst-case scenarios of identity theft and potential financial impact for the customers. Will the reputation of this travel agent recover enough to remain a viable business?

There are generic drivers for SIAM that can be tailored for each organization. These can be placed into five driver groups:

1. Service satisfaction
2. Service and sourcing landscape
3. Operational efficiencies
4. External drivers
5. Commercial drivers

1.5.2.1 Service satisfaction drivers

These are drivers related to the level of satisfaction the customer has with the services that they receive, and the level of satisfaction that is expected.

There are seven drivers related to service satisfaction:

1. Service performance
2. Service provider interactions
3. Clarity of roles and responsibilities
4. Slow pace of change
5. Demonstration of value
6. Lack of collaboration between service providers
7. Delivery silos

Service performance

Customers expect guaranteed service performance and availability, irrespective of who provides the service.

On some occasions, customers in a multi-service provider ecosystem can experience dissatisfaction with the level of service they receive, even though each of the service providers report that they are achieving their individual service level targets.

One example is incident resolution times, where the time taken to pass an incident from one service provider to another is not considered in the service level calculation.

Without effective governance, coordination and collaboration, there will be service performance issues including:

- A lack of transparency for the end-to-end service
- Incomplete understanding of, and inability to report on, end-to-end service performance
- No management of service levels across the end-to-end service
- Service performance that is not aligned to business requirements

Service provider interactions

In a multi-service provider environment, service users might have to interact separately and differently with each internal and external service provider.

For example, one service provider might only accept contact from users by telephone, another only by email, and another only by an internet portal.

Clarity of roles and responsibilities

Roles, responsibilities and accountabilities can be unclear in an ecosystem that has multiple service providers. The responsibility and accountability for the delivery of services is often held in several different places.

Some customer departments may have the primary relationship with a service provider, for example the payroll department with the external provider of payroll services. Some service providers may need to have relationships with multiple customer departments, for example the hosting provider with IT operations, the engineering department and the application development department.

Without effective governance and coordination, a culture can develop where there is no ownership of issues, leading to customer dissatisfaction and loss of perceived value.

For example, a customer frequently experiences slow performance of a business service. This service is underpinned by several technical services from different service providers. Every provider says that its service is performing correctly and another service provider must be responsible.

Slow pace of change

Customers expect changes to be made quickly to meet business requirements.

They also expect that new services, new service providers and new technologies can be introduced rapidly and integrated with existing services to meet demanding timescales.

Demonstration of value

Customers expect that services will deliver the outcomes they require, at a reasonable level of cost and quality. In many organizations, the IT department is not able to demonstrate this value to the customer.

Lack of collaboration between service providers

As the number of parties involved in service delivery increases, so does the need for collaboration.

The requirement is no longer just about a one-way relationship between a service provider and the customer, but a network of relationships between multiple service providers that all need to work together to provide a customer-focused service.

External service providers have their own commercial interests and drivers, which can conflict with the goals of the customer and other service providers.

An example of this is where a business service received by the customer relies on the integration of several services from different service providers. An individual service provider may only be concerned with the availability of the service elements for which it is responsible.

If a service provider does not consider how its service interacts with other providers' services, it could make changes that stop the integrated service working.

Delivery silos

Delivery silos can exist where there are multiple internal or external service providers. Each service provider focuses only on its own goals and outcomes.

These silos isolate service providers, processes and departments. Their impact includes:

- Duplication of work
- Lack of knowledge sharing
- Increased cost of service provision
- Potential for degraded service performance
- Inability to identify service improvements

A blame culture can arise between the service providers due to the lack of cooperation between silos. When a service is faulty, each silo focuses on proving it is not at fault, rather than working with other silos to correct the fault.

1.5.2.2 Service and sourcing landscape drivers

These are drivers related to the nature, number and types of services and service providers, and the complexity of the interactions between them.

There are five drivers related to the service and sourcing landscape:

1. External sourcing
2. Shadow IT
3. Multi-sourcing
4. Increase in the number of service providers
5. Inflexible contracts

External sourcing

Many of the traditional frameworks and practices used to manage IT services were designed for an environment where most of the services were developed and supported internally. However, the way that many customers source their services has fundamentally changed.

Rather than the former insourced approach, many organizations have made the strategic decision to source applications and services externally.

External sourcing of services may enable a customer to reduce costs by realizing the benefits of competition among a wider network of service providers. This sourcing approach can also provide the customer with access to best-in-class capabilities.

These services often include specialized and cloud-based commodity services. The customer expects that all services will be fully integrated with other services that they consume.

Shadow IT

Shadow IT describes IT services and systems commissioned by business departments, without the knowledge of the IT department (sometimes referred to as 'stealth IT').

These services are commissioned to meet a business requirement, but can cause problems when they require connectivity and alignment with the other services consumed by the customer.

Multi-sourcing

Many organizations have made a strategic decision to transition from single-sourcing to multi-sourcing and multiple delivery channels.

This transition often results in a mix of internal and external sourcing. Multi-sourcing can reduce many of the risks and issues associated with being over-reliant on a single service provider. These risks include:

- Slow pace of change and low levels of innovation
- High cost of services when benchmarked against competitors
- Reliance on specific technology platforms
- Inability to take advantage of new service offerings, service providers or technologies that are available elsewhere
- Long-term contractual restrictions
- Lack of control over services
- Lack of service knowledge in the customer organization
- High risk to service continuity during a transition to a new service provider
- Cost of the transition to a new single service provider
- A risk that the service provider may go out of business

Increase in the number of service providers

The number of service providers in the market is increasing. More and more options are available to customer organizations that are evaluating different sourcing approaches.

Inflexible contracts

Lengthy, inflexible contracts with service providers lock in customers and prevent them accessing technology developments and innovative practices.

Moving to a SIAM model will typically include shorter, more flexible contracts that allow customers to add and remove service providers, and adapt how they work with existing service providers.

1.5.2.3 Operational efficiencies drivers

These are drivers that relate to improvements and efficiencies for the end-to-end delivery of services, and the potential to create operational efficiencies through standardization and consolidation.

There are four drivers related to operational efficiencies:

1. Disparate service management capabilities
2. Data and information flows
3. Data and information standards
4. Tooling

Disparate service management capabilities

In an environment with multiple service providers, each of them will maintain its own service management capability. The customer will also need to retain service management capabilities, which interact with the service providers.

This can result in:

- Duplication of resources and activities
- Low utilization in some areas and high utilization in others
- Inconsistent levels of capability and maturity
- No sharing of knowledge
- Inconsistent processes and procedures
- A blame culture between teams

These can result in increased costs and degraded service performance for the customer organization.

Data and information flows

In an environment with multiple service providers, data and information will be transferred between parties during end-to-end service delivery.

If the data and information flows are not mapped and understood, the flow can be interrupted, leading to service performance issues and operational inefficiencies.

The 'integration' element of the SIAM methodology manages the service from end to end. This requires an understanding of all data and information sources and interactions between all parties.[9]

Mapping data and information flows provides an insight into the boundaries between the different service providers. This knowledge can then be used to create integrated flows of data and information.

SIAM is then used to manage and coordinate these flows. This enables end-to-end delivery of the required level of service to the customer.

Data and information standards

If data and information standards are not consistent across all service providers, then extra effort will be required when data and information are exchanged between service providers and with the customer.

A common data dictionary, introduced as part of an integrated approach to service management, would include:

- Incident severity, categorization and recording
- Service levels and service reporting
- Requests for change
- Capacity and availability recording
- Management report formats
- Knowledge artefacts

Tooling

Service providers will have their own toolsets to support their internal processes. When there is a requirement to exchange data and information with other providers and the customer, lack of integration between toolsets can create problems.

Without a design for interoperability, these exchanges can be inefficient, leading to:

- Re-entry of data and information by the receiving party (the 'swivel chair approach')
- A requirement to translate data and information
- Inadvertent alteration of data and information
- Loss of data and information
- Time delays in the exchange between the parties, resulting in a poor service experience

---

[9] Techniques like OBASHI can be used to map data flows to support SIAM.

The swivel chair approach

The 'swivel chair approach'[10] is a colloquial term for manually entering data into one system and then entering the same data into another system. The term is derived from the practice of the user turning from one system to another using a swivel chair.

1.5.2.4 External drivers

These are drivers that are imposed from outside the organization. The organization must respond to these drivers in some way.

There are two drivers related to external factors:

1. Corporate governance
2. External policy

Corporate governance

Many customers have corporate governance requirements that demand clarity over the responsibilities of service providers and the controls that are applied to them. An example is the Sarbanes–Oxley Act passed in the US in 2002 to protect investors from fraudulent accounting activities.

Effective corporate governance requires a definition of roles, responsibilities, accountabilities and interactions between all parties and systems at a far more granular level than in the past.

External policy

For some organizations, the use of SIAM is mandated under a policy created outside the customer organization.

Policy drivers apply to:

- Public-sector organizations affected by government or state policies
- Public-sector service providers affected by government or state policies
- Private-sector organizations that are part of a larger group that has adopted SIAM as part of its strategy

1.5.2.5 Commercial drivers

These drivers apply to organizations that want to offer commercial services related to SIAM.

There are two drivers related to commercial factors:

1. Service providers
2. Service integrators

---

[10] *www.webopedia.com/definitions/swivel-chair-interface/*.

Service providers

When a customer organization adopts SIAM, it will need its service providers to align to its SIAM model.

The delivery models of many traditional providers do not align with SIAM models, because they do not consider the requirements for integration with other service providers and a service integrator.

If these service providers want to be able to compete for business in SIAM ecosystems, they must make changes to how they deliver their services.

Changes will affect:

- Tooling
- Processes and procedures
- Process interfaces
- Data dictionaries and standards
- Service reporting
- Governance approaches
- Data and information standards
- Commercial and contractual standards

Service integrators

Some organizations want to provide service integration capabilities to customers. They might act as an externally sourced or hybrid service integrator, or they might provide specialized support during one or more stages of the SIAM roadmap:

- Discovery & Strategy
- Plan & Build
- Implement
- Run & Improve

1.6 Value to the organization – the SIAM business case

Any organization that is considering a transition to SIAM needs to understand the expected benefits. Clarity on these benefits will form the basis for developing the organization's business case for SIAM.

Benefits can be a mixture of tangible (for example, cost savings) and intangible (for example, improved customer service).

The benefits and costs will be different for each organization. They depend on many factors, including:

- Drivers
- Required business outcomes
- Services in scope
- The customer organization's role in the SIAM ecosystem
- Budget

- Organizational culture
- Appetite for risk
- The legacy contracts in place and their flexibility to accommodate new ways of working

The costs that will be incurred need to include not just cost of service under a SIAM model, but also the cost of the transition project to achieve the change. There will also be costs associated with developing any capabilities or artefacts that the organization does not currently have but that will be required to operate within a SIAM ecosystem.

An organization should consider its own drivers to achieve the necessary clarity for the anticipated business benefits.

There are generic benefits that are likely to be relevant to most organizations making the transition to SIAM.

The benefits can be placed into four groups:

1. Improved service quality
2. Optimized costs and increased value
3. Improved governance and control
4. Improved flexibility and pace

When defining the expected benefits, organizations should consider how long it will take for them to be delivered. It can be some time after the transition is complete before benefits start to be realized.

A SIAM model leverages experience and input from multiple service providers. It delivers benefits from collaboration between service providers, and from competitive tension between them.

1.6.1 Improved service quality

Improving service quality often forms part of a SIAM business case. Benefits related to service quality can include:

- A shift in focus from satisfying contractual targets to focus on innovation and satisfying perceived business need
- Consistent achievement of service levels, including end-to-end:
  - o Incident and problem resolution times
  - o Service availability
  - o Service reliability
- Improvements in customer satisfaction with the services
- The customer being able to concentrate on delivering its business outcomes, and having confidence in its supporting services
- Improved quality in the delivery of changes, integrated across service providers
- Improved flow of end-to-end processes, sometimes referred to as 'SIAM cadence'
- Consistency in how end users interact with service providers
- Consistent and understandable management information about the services
- Access to best-of-breed services and service providers

- Development and sharing of knowledge and best practice
- Continual service improvement

1.6.2 Optimized costs and improved value

The business case for SIAM must include the costs associated with the transition to a new way of working. The service integrator layer can add additional cost to an organization, whether it is sourced externally or provisioned using internal resources.

However, the increased value associated with a transition to SIAM, and the potential for cost optimization in the service provider layer, should balance out or exceed any overall cost increases.

If SIAM is correctly designed and implemented, it will provide better service value, with both tangible and intangible benefits.

Benefits in this group include:

- Cost optimization from:
  - Innovation
  - An understanding of the true cost and value of each service and service provider
  - Competitive tension between service providers
  - Best use of skilled (and often scarce) resource
  - Reduced costs of process execution
  - Identification and removal of duplication of resources and activities
- Improved value for money for individual services
- Consistent performance from all service providers, leading to improved efficiency
- Improved management of resources and capacity
- Faster response to changing business needs
- Faster access to new technologies and services
- Contract optimization and the potential for shorter-term, more effective contracts
- The flexibility to accommodate change

1.6.3 Improved governance and control

SIAM provides an opportunity to apply consistent governance and control over all service providers, both internal and external.

Governance and control benefits include:

- Consistent and visible definition and application of a governance framework
- Consistent assurance of services and service providers
- A single point of ownership, visibility and control of services
- Clearly defined services, roles, responsibilities and controls
- Improved management of service provider performance
- The ability to benchmark between service providers
- Contract optimization and standardization related to governance and control
- Improved visibility, understanding and management of service risks

1.6.4 Improved flexibility

If correctly designed and implemented, SIAM can provide the flexibility that is necessary to support changing business requirements, balanced with an appropriate level of control.

The benefits in this group include:

- Effective and timely introduction of new and changed services and service providers
- The flexibility to replace poorly performing or uneconomic service providers
- The ability to rapidly accommodate changes to services, technologies and business requirements
- Increased ability to manage commodity services in a consistent way
- Increased ability to scale service provision

CHAPTER 2: SIAM ROADMAP

This roadmap outlines an example plan for the implementation of SIAM as part of an organization's operating model.

Using a roadmap for the implementation has several benefits, including:

- Defining the SIAM requirements
- Providing a planning framework
- Determining the most appropriate SIAM structure and SIAM model
- Guiding the implementation
- Directing ongoing continual improvement

There are four stages in the SIAM roadmap:

1. Discovery & Strategy
2. Plan & Build
3. Implement
4. Run & Improve

For each stage, this section provides examples of:

1. Objectives
2. Triggers
3. Inputs
4. Activities
5. Outputs

While the activities are presented here in a sequential manner, many are likely to be iterative or may even be undertaken in parallel.

High-level requirements are defined in the first stage. These are then further developed in the second stage, before being implemented in the third stage. The fourth stage is where the SIAM model is operated and continually improved.

In many cases, the roadmap will be executed iteratively, with a checkpoint at the end of each stage. The checkpoint should review areas including:

- The actual outputs from the stage against those intended
- Risks
- Issues
- Plan for the next stage

This information should be used to validate decisions taken earlier in the roadmap. It might highlight potential issues, requiring a return to an earlier stage for further work.

An example of an iterative roadmap

In the Discovery & Strategy stage, a customer organization might propose an internally sourced service integrator.

In the second stage, it formulates a plan and designs its SIAM model to support this structure.

However, during the third stage, it discovers that it is unable to recruit the necessary resources. It returns to the first stage to review its strategy, and changes it to apply the hybrid service integrator structure.

The Plan & Build stage must then be revisited.

Many organizations use outside assistance during the execution of their SIAM roadmap. This can be helpful during the transition to SIAM, but the customer organization needs to ensure that the model being used by the external organization is suitable for its needs.

If outside help is required, it is a good idea to have a commercial boundary between an organization that is assisting with the Discovery & Strategy and Plan & Build stages, and any external service integrator.

2.1 Discovery & Strategy

2.1.1 Objectives

The Discovery & Strategy stage initiates the SIAM transformation project, formulates key strategies, and maps the current situation. This enables the customer organization to:

- Determine what it intends to source internally
- Consider any additional skills and resources that may be required
- Determine what it would like to source externally
- Understand the expected benefits

The objectives for this stage are to:

- Establish the SIAM transition project
- Establish a governance framework
- Define the strategy and outline model for SIAM and the services in scope
- Analyze the current state of the organization, including skills, services, service providers, tools and processes
- Analyze the marketplace for potential service providers and service integrators

2.1.2 Triggers

There are many reasons organizations should consider adopting a SIAM model. These drivers are described in **section 1.5.2**.

2.1.3 Inputs

Inputs to this stage include:

- Enterprise, corporate and IT governance standards
- Current business, procurement and IT strategies
- Business requirements and constraints
- Current organization structure, processes, products and practices
- Existing service provider information, including existing contracts and agreements
- Understanding of market forces and technology trends

2.1.4 Activities

The activities in this stage are:

1. Establish the project
2. Define strategic objectives
3. Define governance requirements and the high-level governance framework
4. Define principles and policies for roles and responsibilities
5. Map the existing services and sourcing environment
6. Assess the organization's current maturity and capability
7. Understand the marketplace
8. Define the strategy for SIAM and the outline SIAM model
9. Produce the outline business case

2.1.4.1 Activity: Establish the project

The SIAM transformation project should be formally established using the organization's selected project management methodology.

This includes:

- Setting up a project management office
- Defining roles and responsibilities for the project
- Setting up project governance
- Agreeing the approach for managing project risks

The organization will also choose whether to adopt a waterfall or Agile project delivery approach.

2.1.4.2 Activity: Define strategic objectives

Strategic objectives are the long-term goals of the organization that SIAM is intended to support.

They are related to the drivers for SIAM and the SIAM business case. The objectives defined and agreed in this activity will be used as a basis for items including the:

- SIAM model
- SIAM governance framework
- Sourcing model

- Roles and responsibilities

2.1.4.3 Activity: Define governance requirements and the high-level governance framework

SIAM requires a specific governance framework that allows the customer organization to exercise and maintain authority over the SIAM ecosystem.

The model should be tailored to the specific SIAM structures, the SIAM model, and the customer organization's overall appetite for risk.

At this stage, the SIAM governance framework will be defined at a high level. It should include:

- Specific corporate governance requirements that support any external regulations and legal requirements
- Controls to be retained and operated by the customer organization
- A definition of governance boards and governance board structures
- Segregation of duties between the customer organization and external organizations
- The risk management approach
- The performance management approach
- The contract management approach
- The dispute management approach

2.1.4.4 Activity: Define principles and policies for roles and responsibilities

In this activity, the key principles and policies for roles and responsibilities are created. They will take into account the governance requirements and strategic objectives.

The specific, detailed roles and responsibilities will not be defined or assigned until more detailed process models and sourcing agreements have been designed within the Plan & Build stage.

Two aspects should be considered here:

- Segregation of duties if one organization is operating in more than one SIAM layer
- Boundaries of delegated authority

2.1.4.5 Activity: Map the existing services and sourcing environment

Before a SIAM model can be designed, the current environment must be understood. This includes:

- Existing services and the service hierarchy
- Existing service providers (internal and external)
- Contracts
- Service provider performance
- Relationships with service providers
- Cost of services

The creation of the service hierarchy is a critical activity to support the design of the desired future state. The hierarchy enables the identification of essential business functions, critical service assets and dependencies across the ecosystem.

This activity will provide clarity on the current environment. It can also help to highlight issues including:

- Duplications in service offerings
- Misaligned contractual commitments
- Unused operational services
- Uneconomic services
- Service risks that require mitigation

Information about service providers can be used to decide whether they are to be retained in the current format, or whether their services should be sourced under new arrangements.

2.1.4.6 Activity: Assess the organization's current maturity and capability

---

Capability: *"The power or ability to do something."*[11]

Maturity: *"Maturity relates to the degree of formality and optimization of processes, from ad hoc practices, to formally defined steps, to managed result metrics, to active optimization of the processes."*[12]

Both **capability** and **maturity** need to be assessed to inform the strategy for SIAM.

For example: a customer organization may currently have low maturity in service integration processes, practices, and tools, but have a high capability in these areas. This may influence its choice of preferred SIAM structure, leading it to select an internally sourced service integrator.

A baselining exercise should be carried out to understand the customer organization's current capability and maturity in organization, processes, practices and tools. This will inform the next stage of the roadmap.

This exercise can also identify any issues that require a review of earlier decisions. For example, where there is insufficient capability to run the project management office, or insufficient maturity of the incident management process.

2.1.4.7 Activity: Understand the marketplace

It is important at this stage to understand the existence and capabilities of potential external service integrators and service providers. This will inform the strategy for SIAM and the SIAM model.

---

[11] *www.lexico.com/definition/capability*.

[12] Capability Maturity Model (CMM), *https://en.wikipedia.org/wiki/Capability_Maturity_Model*.

This activity should include a review of available technologies and services against the strategic objectives.

For example, a move to cloud services can support a strategic objective for reduced cost of ownership.

The service providers of commodity cloud services are unlikely to take part in the SIAM model's boards, process forums and working groups. This could reduce the workload of the service integrator, to a level where an internally sourced service integrator may offer better value than an externally sourced service integrator.

2.1.4.8 Activity: Define the strategy for SIAM and the outline SIAM model

This activity will take the information and outputs from previous activities in this stage to define the strategy for SIAM, and an outline SIAM model.

These should include:

Strategy for SIAM:

- The vision for SIAM
- Strategic objectives
- Current maturity and capability
- Existing services and sourcing environment
- Marketplace analysis
- Governance requirements
- Proposed SIAM structure, including retained capabilities
- Proposed sourcing approach
- Justification for proposals

Outline SIAM model

- Principles and policies
- Governance framework
- Outline roles and responsibilities
- Outline of process models, practices and structural elements
- Outline of services
- Service providers to be retired

The strategy for SIAM and the chosen SIAM model both need to align with the original business requirements and the business strategy.

2.1.4.9 Activity: Produce the outline business case

This activity will take the information and outputs from all previous activities in this stage to produce an outline business case for SIAM.

This should include:

- Strategy for SIAM

- Outline SIAM model
- Current state
- Expected benefits from SIAM
- Risks
- Outline costs of the transition to SIAM
- High-level plan

The outline business case should be approved in accordance with the customer organization's governance arrangements before the next roadmap stage begins.

2.1.5 Outputs

The outputs from the Discovery & Strategy stage are:

- An established SIAM transition project;
- Strategic objectives
- Governance requirements and a high-level SIAM governance framework
- Defined principles and policies for roles and responsibilities
- A map of existing services and the sourcing environment
- Current maturity and capability levels
- Market awareness
- An approved outline business case for SIAM
- A strategy for SIAM
- An outline SIAM model

2.2 Plan & Build

2.2.1 Objectives

The Plan & Build stage builds on the outputs from the Discovery & Strategy stage to complete the design for SIAM and create the plans for the transformation.

During this stage, all plans and approvals are put in place before the Implement stage begins. The main objectives for this stage are to:

- Complete the design of the SIAM model, including the services that are in scope
- Obtain full approval for the SIAM model
- Appoint the service integrator and service providers
- Commence organizational change management

2.2.2 Triggers

This stage is triggered on completion of the Discovery & Strategy stage, when the organization confirms its intention to proceed with a SIAM implementation.

2.2.3 Inputs

The inputs to this stage are the outline business case, and the high-level model and frameworks created during the Discovery & Strategy stage:

- Governance requirements and high-level SIAM governance framework
- Defined principles and policies for roles and responsibilities
- Map of existing services and sourcing environment
- Current maturity and capability levels
- Market awareness
- Approved outline business case for SIAM
- Strategy for SIAM
- Outline SIAM model

In this stage, work will be carried out to further define, refine and add detail to the outputs from the previous stage. Some organizations may choose to use an Agile approach for this.

2.2.4 Activities

The activities during this stage are:

1. Design the detailed SIAM model
2. Approve the full business case
3. Commence organizational change management
4. Appoint the service integrator
5. Appoint service providers
6. Plan for service provider and service retirement
7. Review stage and approve implementation

2.2.4.1 Activity: Design the detailed SIAM model

The SIAM model provides the detail for how SIAM will be applied across all parties in the SIAM ecosystem. It contains many elements, including:

1. Service model and sourcing approach
2. The selected SIAM structure
3. Process models
4. Governance model
5. Detailed roles and responsibilities
6. Performance management and reporting framework
7. Collaboration model
8. Tooling strategy
9. Ongoing improvement framework

Careful design of this model is critical to success. The design activities will not necessarily be sequential. There is more likely to be an iterative cycle, which starts with an initial definition, and becomes successively more detailed as each iteration is agreed.

There must be regular review and feedback across all the design activities. Agile approaches can be particularly useful for this. Consideration must also be given to interdependencies between the different design activities.

Organizations will determine the level of detail they require for their own SIAM model. This will depend on several factors, including:

- Strategic objectives
- Market conditions
- Services and service complexity
- Number of service providers
- Appetite for risk
- Resource and process capability and maturity
- Available tools
- Budget

2.2.4.1.1 Define service model and sourcing approach

This activity defines the services in scope for the SIAM model, the service hierarchy, and how the services are grouped for sourcing. Creating the service model is a critical activity for an effective transition to SIAM.

These areas must be clearly defined for each service:

- The service provider(s)
- The service consumer(s)
- The service characteristics, including service levels
- The service boundaries
- Dependencies with other services
- Technical interactions with other services
- Data and information interactions with other services
- Service outcomes, value and objectives

Services should be placed into groups, with groups assigned to specific service providers. The service model shows the hierarchy of the proposed services, and the service provider for each service. This forms part of the overall SIAM model.

The model should also include the expected process interactions between the services and service providers. Enabling practices like OBASHI[13] can support this by mapping data flows between service providers.

The service model will help to identify omissions, single points of failure, and duplication.

---

[13] For more information, visit: *https://obashi.co.uk/*.

The aim should be to achieve a balance between getting 'best of breed' services, the number of services and service providers, and the complexity of the service model and hierarchy. There also needs to be a balance between service complexity and integration complexity. Services should be designed to minimize interactions with other services, as these interactions drive complexity, risk, and cost.

Care should be taken when defining the services and assigning them to service providers. The number of contact points and interactions, and therefore opportunities for failure, will increase as the number of services and service providers increase.

Sourcing approach for services

The ability to source services in groups is one of the benefits of SIAM. Rather than having a single, monolithic contract with one service provider delivering everything, the full range of services can be broken down into the most efficient and best-value groupings. Each group is then individually sourced, externally or internally.

Common examples of service groups include:

- Hosting
- Application development and support
- Desktop support/end-user computing
- Networks
- Cloud services
- Managed services

Each group can be provided by one or more service providers. For example, a 'hosting' group could include Platform as a Service (PaaS) and Infrastructure as a Service (IaaS), sourced from one or multiple service providers.

The design of service groups should try to minimize any technical dependencies between services. Dependencies create interactions between service providers and potential points of failure, and can increase the workload of the service integrator.

There is no requirement within the SIAM management methodology to separate services that logically stay together. For example, there is no need to divide a SaaS offering into 'hosting' and 'application development and support' if it is more logical to source it as one group.

Unnecessary separation can cause issues, such as disputes about who is responsible for performance problems. This particularly applies to managed services, legacy services, cloud services and DevOps services.

There is no limit to the number of different groups within a SIAM model. However, integration complexity will increase as the number of service groups increases.

2.2.4.1.2 Select the SIAM structure

The selected SIAM structure determines the sourcing approach for the service integrator. This is a crucial decision that must be taken with care, as any changes to the structure after this point will result in rework and cost.

All the information gathered so far should be used to select the preferred SIAM structure. If this is different from the proposal created during the Discovery & Strategy stage, it may be necessary to repeat parts of that stage.

See **section 3** for more information on the advantages and disadvantages of each structure.

2.2.4.1.3 Design process models

In a SIAM model, the execution of most processes will involve multiple service providers. Each service provider might carry out individual steps in a different way, but as part of an overall integrated process model.

Process models are therefore important SIAM artefacts; the individual processes and work instructions are likely to remain within the domain of the individual service providers.

The process model for each process should describe:

- Purpose and outcomes
- High-level activities
- Inputs, outputs, interactions and dependencies with other processes
- Inputs, outputs and interactions between the different parties (for example, between the service providers and the service integrator)
- Controls
- Measures
- Supporting policies and templates

Techniques such as swim lane models, RACI matrices, and process mapping are commonly used, and are helpful for establishing and communicating process models.

The process models will continue to evolve and improve as further activities are undertaken in this stage, and in the Run & Improve stage. This includes getting input from the selected service providers and service integrator.

Adding granularity

The iterative design and development of the SIAM structure, services and service groups, roles and responsibilities, governance model, process models, performance management and reporting framework, collaboration model, tooling strategy and ongoing improvement framework all add detail to the SIAM model.

This detailed work and an iterative approach is critical to ensure that the SIAM model will work once implemented, and that it aligns with the strategy for SIAM and the customer organization's requirements.

2.2.4.1.4 Design governance model

The governance model should be designed using the governance framework and the roles and responsibilities. For each governance body, this model should include:

- Scope
- Accountabilities
- Responsibilities
- Meeting formats
- Meeting frequencies
- Inputs
- Outputs (including reports)
- Hierarchy
- Terms of reference
- Related policies

The governance framework should also be updated and more detail added. This is an iterative activity that should be completed before the end of this roadmap stage.

2.2.4.1.5 Design roles and responsibilities

Roles and responsibilities should be designed using the outline SIAM model and outline process models, the SIAM structure and the governance framework.

This should include the detailed design and allocation of roles and responsibilities to:

- Process models
- Practices
- Governance boards
- Process forums
- Working groups
- Organizational structures and locations for any retained capabilities

This work may highlight a need to review earlier designs and decisions.

Roles and responsibilities can be further developed in the Run & Improve stage, but the detail must be confirmed in this stage before any service integrator or service providers can be appointed.

2.2.4.1.6 Design performance management and reporting framework

The performance management and reporting framework for SIAM addresses measuring and reporting on a range of items including:

- Key performance indicators
- Performance of processes and process models
- Achievement of service level targets
- System and service performance
- Adherence to contractual and non-contractual responsibilities
- Collaboration
- Customer satisfaction

Measurements should be taken for each service provider and its services, but also across the end-to-end SIAM ecosystem.

Designing an appropriate performance management and reporting framework for a SIAM ecosystem can be challenging. It is usually straightforward to measure the performance of an individual service provider; the challenge is in measuring end-to-end performance as experienced by the users, particularly when there may be limited consistency in how each of the providers measure and report.

The framework should also include the standards for:

- Data classification
- Reporting formats and frequency

2.2.4.1.7 Design collaboration model

SIAM can only be effective when service providers, the service integrator and the customer can communicate and collaborate with each other.

Section 7 has some examples of how to encourage collaboration in SIAM ecosystems.

2.2.4.1.8 Define tooling strategy

A consistent and comprehensive tooling strategy is important within a SIAM ecosystem. The tooling strategy is influenced by:

- The selected SIAM structure
- The SIAM model
- Existing customer toolsets
- Service provider and service integrator toolsets
- Types of service provider
- Budget

The tooling strategy should focus on supporting the flow of data and information and process integration efficiently:

- Between the service providers
- Between service providers and the service integrator
- Between the service integrator and the customer

This is more important than focusing on technology alone.

Many organizations use more than one toolset in their SIAM ecosystem, selecting a range of 'best of breed' toolsets for:

- Supporting service management processes
- Data analysis
- Reporting and presentation
- Event monitoring
- Audit logging

There are four main options for toolsets:

1. A single toolset is used by all parties, mandated by the customer
2. The service providers use their own toolsets and integrate them with the service integrator's toolset
3. The service providers use their own toolsets and the service integrator integrates them with its own toolset
4. An integration service is used to incorporate the toolsets of the service providers and the service integrator

The tooling strategy should include:

- Enterprise architecture
- Functional and non-functional requirements
- Integration requirements (technical and logical)
- Data mapping for each SIAM layer
- Data ownership
- Access control
- Measurement and reporting

2.2.4.1.9 Design ongoing improvement framework

An improvement framework needs to be developed and maintained in conjunction with all parties within the SIAM model. This will ensure a focus on continual improvement across the SIAM ecosystem.

Service providers should have incentives that encourage them to suggest and deliver improvements and innovation.

2.2.4.2 Activity: Approve full business case

At this point, the design should be detailed and complete enough to enable the full costs of the SIAM transition and the anticipated benefits to be determined.

The outline business case should be reviewed and updated with detailed information to create a full business case.

This should then be approved using the organization's corporate governance and approvals process. The approval allows the start of procurement activities for any external service providers, service integrator, and tools.

2.2.4.3 Activity: Commence organizational change management

A SIAM transformation is a major business change, affecting the customer organization, service integrator and service providers at every level.

Organizational change management will be essential if the transformation is to succeed.

During any organizational change, it is important to protect the existing service and minimize the impact on the existing organization.

2.2.4.4 Activity: Appoint the service integrator

Ideally, the service integrator should be selected and in place before the SIAM model is finalized and before any service providers are selected.

If this can be achieved, the service integrator can be involved with the Plan & Build activities. The benefits of this approach are:

- The service integrator is involved with the design and selection of service providers, so it can use its experience to assist with these activities
- The service integrator is fully aware of the requirements placed on the service providers during selection and appointment

The selection process and contractual agreement for an external service integrator may take some time. On occasion, the customer might source the service integrator and the service providers simultaneously.

Alternatively, the service providers might already be in place or undergoing transition from legacy contracts before the service integrator role is confirmed.

2.2.4.5 Activity: Appoint service providers

Service providers cannot be selected until this point, as it will not be possible to fully document the requirements until the SIAM model has been fully defined.

The contracts in place in a SIAM model need to support the overall strategy for SIAM. It is important to ensure that they include appropriate targets and risk and reward models. Detailed requirements should be included in any contracts or internal agreements.

Cloud services

Where cloud services have been selected, requirements often need to be adjusted to consider that these are commodity services.

For example, cloud commodity service providers are unlikely to take part in boards, process forums or working groups; to change their processes; or to integrate their toolsets with others.

The challenge is to balance the customer's desire for specific requirements against what is offered in the marketplace. Forcing service providers to customize their delivery models can result in increased costs and risks.

The procurement of external service providers can take some time, which needs to be included in any plan or timeline.

It is important to verify that the desired service providers can meet the full set of requirements in the SIAM model, particularly for strategic service providers. If there are issues or gaps, this may require a return to earlier lifecycle stages and activities.

In addition to the service providers that are appointed here, it is important to remember that service providers can be added and removed throughout the SIAM roadmap. Some service providers may not be appointed until after a legacy contract has expired.

2.2.4.6 Activity: Plan for service provider and service retirement

Planning also needs to address retiring services, and any resulting transfer of services to new service providers.

The relationships with any service providers, service dependencies, contract end dates and potential impact of retiring a particular service or service provider must be carefully considered.

Detailed plans should be developed for any decommissioning, discontinuation, and transfer of services. The plans need to include contractual restrictions, legal requirements, and lead times for service termination.

They must also detail how data, information, and knowledge will be transferred from retiring service providers, including:

- What needs to be transferred
- To whom it will be transferred
- When it needs to be transferred
- How to assess if the transfer is successful

2.2.4.7 Activity: Review stage and approve implementation

The outputs from this stage should be reviewed against decisions taken in the previous stage, to identify if there are any issues or necessary changes. The roadmap will then progress to the Implement stage if approval is given.

2.2.5 Outputs

The outputs from the Plan & Build stage are:

- Full design of the SIAM model including:
  - Services, service groups and service providers (the 'service model')
  - The selected SIAM structure
  - Process models
  - Practices
  - Structural elements
  - Roles and responsibilities
  - Governance model
  - Performance management and reporting framework
  - Collaboration model
  - Tooling strategy
  - Ongoing improvement framework
- Approved business case
- Organizational change management activities
- Service integrator appointed
- Service providers appointed
- A plan for service provider and service retirement

There may be several iterations during this stage before the outputs are complete and the roadmap progresses to the next stage. The outputs from Plan & Build must be detailed enough to support the implementation activities.

2.3 Implement

2.3.1 Objectives

The objective of this stage is to manage the transition from the organization's 'as is' current state to the 'to be' desired future state, the new SIAM model. At the end of this stage, the new SIAM model will be in place and in use.

2.3.2 Triggers

This stage is triggered when the organization completes all activities in the Discovery & Strategy and Plan & Build stages.

The timing for the start of the Implement stage can be influenced by events in the existing environment. For example, implementation could be triggered by:

- The end of an existing service provider's contract
- An existing service provider ceasing to trade
- Organizational structure changes due to corporate restructure or takeover

The customer organization may have limited control over the timing of these events. It may need to react to them by completing as many of the Discovery & Strategy and Plan & Build activities as possible. There will be an increased level of risk if the activities from these stages are not fully completed owing to a lack of time.

2.3.3 Inputs

All the outputs from the Discovery & Strategy and Plan & Build stages form inputs for the Implement stage.

2.3.4 Activities

The activities in this stage focus on making the transition to the new SIAM model. They include:

1. Select the implementation approach
2. Transition to the approved SIAM model
3. Ongoing organizational change management

2.3.4.1 Activity: Select the implementation approach

There are two possible approaches to implementation:

1. 'Big bang'
2. Phased

2.3.4.1.1 'Big bang' implementation

A 'big bang' implementation approach is one that introduces everything at once, including the service integrator, service providers (with new contracts) and new ways of working.

The 'big bang' approach can be high risk, because it affects the entire organization at the same time. The resulting impact on the customer's business and the services provided can be very high, unless the risks are planned for and carefully managed.

Most organizations that adopt SIAM are introducing it into an environment with existing providers, contracts and relationships.

This can mean that 'big bang' is not possible, as different contracts expire at different times. The 'big bang' approach does provide an opportunity to make a 'clean break' from all legacy issues and behaviors at the same time and avoids the complexities of managing a phased approach.

2.3.4.1.2 Phased implementation

A phased implementation approach makes the transformation to the new SIAM model in smaller, more easily manageable transition projects and iterations. This can be achieved in several ways, including:

- One service at a time
- One service provider at a time
- One practice at a time
- One process at a time

This phased approach to SIAM implementation can lower the level of risk associated with the transition, but can be more complex to manage and will extend the total time for implementation.

Specific care needs to be given to define and understand the impact of each transition and to ensure that the delivery of existing services continues with no disruption.

2.3.4.2 Activity: Transition to the approved SIAM model

The transition activities will be dependent on the selected approach: phased or 'big bang'.

This activity involves:

- Establishing processes and supporting infrastructure
- Commencing transition activity to new service providers and services
- Removing service providers who are not part of the SIAM model
- Verifying the successful execution of the transition steps
- Toolset and process alignment between all parties

This is not a trivial activity. The number of service providers, services, processes and toolsets will all affect the complexity of the transition. It involves the transition to the full SIAM model, including the implementation of new:

- Service providers
- Services
- Service integrator
- Process models
- Roles and responsibilities
- Tools
- Practices
- Structural elements
- Contracts and agreements
- Governance framework
- Performance management and reporting framework

A robust methodology should be used for this transition, including:

- Testing (both functional and non-functional)
- Data migration
- Service introduction
- Deployment testing
- Service acceptance
- Post-transition support

The transition normally requires resources who are specifically dedicated to and focused on it.

The service providers selected during Plan & Build will need to be transferred into the SIAM ecosystem as part of the Implement stage.

Existing service providers that are taking on a new role in the SIAM ecosystem will need to understand fully their new role, relationships and interfaces. New service providers will need to undergo transition into the ecosystem in a managed way.

This activity should be managed by the service integrator on behalf of the customer. It is vital that clear ownership and roles and responsibilities are agreed, including reporting lines, escalation paths and mandates to ensure efficient and effective decision-making.

2.3.4.3 Activity: Ongoing organizational change management

Organizational change management started in the Plan & Build stage of the roadmap. It continues through this stage and into the next.

Specific activities in the Implement stage include:

- Conducting awareness campaigns throughout the organization
- Communicating with and preparing stakeholders for the change
- Ensuring appropriate training is completed
- Continuing with deployment of the organizational change plans
- Measuring the effectiveness of communications and organizational change activities

It is important to focus on protecting the existing service and minimizing organizational impact during this stage.

2.3.5 Outputs

The output from the Implement stage is the new SIAM model that is in place and operating, and supported by appropriate contracts and agreements.

2.4 Run & Improve

2.4.1 Objectives

The objectives of the Run & Improve stage include:

- Manage the SIAM model
- Manage day-to-day service delivery
- Manage processes, teams and tools
- Manage the continual improvement activities

2.4.2 Triggers

This stage is triggered when the Implement stage is completed. If the chosen implementation approach is 'phased', Run & Improve will take over elements of delivery in an incremental way, as each phase, service, process or service provider exits the Implement stage.

2.4.3 Inputs

Inputs to this stage will include:

- The SIAM model
- Process models
- Performance management and reporting framework
- Collaboration model for providers
- Tooling strategy
- Ongoing improvement framework

These inputs have been designed during the Discovery & Strategy and Plan & Build stages, and then transferred during the Implement stage.

2.4.4 Activities

The activities in this stage focus on providing consistent, guaranteed service outcomes to the business, which can be managed, measured and improved. They include:

1. Operate governance structural elements
2. Performance management and improvement
3. Operate management structural elements
4. Audit and compliance
5. Reward
6. Ongoing change management

> In the Run & Improve stage, the new operating model should no longer be seen as 'new'; it is just how things are done.

2.4.4.1 Activity: Operate governance structural elements

Governance boards provide an important role in the control of the overall SIAM ecosystem.

During the Plan & Build stage, the high-level governance framework was created. In Implement, it was transferred to the live environment. In Run & Improve, governance board members adopt their new roles.

See **sections 5** and **1** for more information about governance boards.

2.4.4.2 Activity: Performance management and improvement

The performance of all services and processes should be measured and monitored against key performance indicators and, where appropriate, service level targets. The measurements should be both qualitative and quantitative.

Measurements are used to create meaningful and understandable reports for the appropriate audiences. They provide visibility of performance issues, and support trend analysis to give early warning of possible failures.

Routine service improvement activities should include review and management of actions arising from the information and review of report relevance.

Within SIAM, reports also need to include feedback for how the service is perceived by users, referred to as qualitative reporting. For more information, see section **6**.

Reports can be used to identify opportunities for improvement and innovation.

2.4.4.3 Activity: Operate management structural elements

Process forums and working groups are two of the structural elements that unite the service integrator, service providers and the customer.

They provide an environment to work collaboratively on the operation of a specific process or processes, process outputs, issue or project.

In this stage of the roadmap, these forums and groups should be actively working. The frequency and format of meetings will vary, but it is a good idea to have regular contact between the forum and group members in the early stages of implementation, as they will be instrumental in creating the necessary collaborative culture.

See sections **5**, **7** and **1** for more information about process forums and working groups.

2.4.4.4 Activity: Audit and compliance

In addition to the review of reports that takes place in a SIAM environment, a more formal audit schedule should also be introduced.

This can include process audits, service audits, service provider audits – whatever is most appropriate for each organization and the SIAM ecosystem.

Some audits will be mandated by regulations, legislation or corporate governance.

These audits may be performed by an external organization.

Audits support ongoing assurance of compliance with the customer organization's legislative and regulatory requirements. They can provide valuable information about whether elements of the model are working as they should and help to embed a culture of improvement.

2.4.4.5 Activity: Reward

A SIAM ecosystem can challenge all stakeholders to behave in new ways. Service providers must be encouraged to collaborate rather than protect their own interests. Reward mechanisms can be used to encourage collaboration and communication.

Good practices for creating a reward system include:

- Using small rewards often, linked to specific actions
- Giving rewards at unexpected times
- Rewarding the behavior, not just the results
- Rewarding all stakeholders, not just one layer of the SIAM model
- Rewarding publicly

Case study

One customer organization has created a CIO Award for Collaboration.

This is given quarterly to the service provider that has demonstrated excellent behaviors, including collaboration, willingness to help others and ease of working with them. The scores are collated and shared with all parties.

Crucially, service providers are encouraged to nominate each other, encouraging them to recognize good behavior within the service provider layer.

2.4.4.6 Activity: Ongoing change management

After the SIAM model enters the Run & Improve stage, it will change and evolve as the sourcing landscape and business requirements change and evolve.

Ongoing change management will include the addition and removal of service providers, scaling the services if customer needs grow or shrink, and potentially changing the SIAM structure.

If major change is required, this can include going back to earlier roadmap stages, for example to revisit Discovery & Strategy.

2.4.5 Outputs

Outputs from the Run & Improve stage fall into two categories:

- **Run outputs:** business-as-usual outputs including reports, service data and process data
- **Improve outputs:** information used to evolve and continually improve the SIAM model

CHAPTER 3: SIAM STRUCTURES

There are four common structures for a SIAM ecosystem. The difference between each structure is the sourcing and configuration of the service integrator layer.

The structures are:

- Externally sourced
- Internally sourced
- Hybrid
- Lead supplier

The customer organization will choose a structure based on factors including:

- Business requirements
- Internal capabilities (including maturity, resources and skills)
- Complexity of the customer's services
- The customer's organizational structure and size
- The legislative and regulatory environment
- Customer budget
- Current organizational maturity and capability in service integration and IT
- Appetite for external sourcing/loss of direct control
- Required timescales
- Appetite for risk
- Types and numbers of service providers to be managed

3.1 Externally sourced service integrator

In this structure, the customer appoints an external organization to take the role and provide the capabilities of the service integrator.

The service provider roles are performed by external service providers and/or internal service providers.

The externally sourced service integrator is exclusively focused on service integration activities and does not take any of the service provider roles, as illustrated in **figure 9**.

Figure 9: Externally sourced service integrator

3.1.1 When does a customer use this structure?

This structure is suitable when the customer organization does not have in-house service integration capabilities and does not intend to develop them.

It is also commonly chosen by organizations that do not have the resources available to take on the service integrator role, and do not want to have an increased headcount or the management responsibilities associated with selecting and maintaining service integration resources.

This structure is suitable for customers that are prepared for another organization to take the service integrator role, and who are prepared to have a high degree of trust in their external service integrator.

It relies on the customer empowering the service integrator and giving it the responsibilities of day-to-day coordination and control of service providers, implementing and coordinating processes and managing end-to-end reporting.

For this structure to succeed, the customer needs retained capabilities to provide strong governance over the external service integrator. These capabilities will identify the goals and the mandate for the external service integrator, and will communicate them clearly to all stakeholders.

The customer must allow the service integrator to act on its behalf. The customer should not bypass the service integrator by having direct operational relationships with the service providers.

Summary: Externally sourced

Suitable for:

- Customers that are prepared for another organization to take the service integrator role
- Customers that are prepared to place a high degree of trust in an external organization acting as their service integrator
- Customers that do not have service integration capabilities and do not want to develop them
- Customers that do not have service integration resources and do not want to add or manage them

3.1.2 Advantages

The advantages of an externally sourced service integrator include:

- The opportunity for the customer to review multiple service integrators and then select an experienced service integrator with good reviews from previous clients.
- The potential for faster benefits realization, as the service integrator's expertise reduces the time to implement the SIAM roadmap, although the time required to select the external service integrator also needs to be considered.
- The potential for improved value, as the service integrator applies its experience to manage the SIAM ecosystem in an efficient and effective way.
- Separation of concerns: the service integrator can focus on the end-to-end governance and coordination of the service, processes, metrics and reporting, and the customer organization can focus on business outcomes and strategic objectives.
- Access to established SIAM models, processes and toolsets, where the service integrator is providing the toolset.
- Access to innovative practices from the service integrator's experience on other SIAM implementations.

3.1.3 Disadvantages

The disadvantages of an externally sourced service integrator include:

- The high level of dependency on the external service integrator adds a level of risk, including commercial, continuity and security risks.
- The potential for higher costs related to the sourcing and management of an external organization
- The potential for resentment from any internal service provider that is part of the customer organization but is being managed by an external organization.
- The potential for resentment from the external service providers in the SIAM ecosystem, particularly where the service providers and service integrator compete in other markets. This can lead to relationship issues and poor performance.
- The external service integrator's models and practices might not be the best fit for the customer organization.

- The use of an external service integrator can make it more difficult to change how the service integrator is working, because contractual changes may be required. This means the customer will be less agile and may result in higher cost.
- There is a risk that the customer decides to appoint an external service integrator because they do not fully understand SIAM themselves. This is likely to increase overall costs of delivery and result in poor service because the customer has not clearly defined its own objectives.
- The time and effort required for the external service integrator to build relationships with the customer organization and with the service providers, which is often not accounted for in the initial investment analysis.
- The service integrator does not have a contractual relationship with the service providers, so without empowerment from the customer, they can be ineffective.

3.2 Internally sourced service integrator

In this SIAM structure, the customer organization takes the role of service integrator, providing the service integration capability. The service integrator role and the customer role still need to be defined and managed separately.

If the customer role and the service integrator role become inseparable and indistinct, service providers may interact with the customer as if it was part of a traditional outsourced ecosystem. The benefits of moving to a SIAM model would not be realized.

The service provider roles are performed by external service providers and/or internal service providers.

The internally sourced service integrator is exclusively focused on service integration activities.

Figure 10 shows the internally sourced service integrator structure.

Figure 10: Internally sourced service integrator

3.2.1 When does a customer use this structure?

This structure is suitable for organizations where the customer already has or intends to develop in-house service integration capabilities.

It is typically used where the customer wants to retain control and flexibility over the SIAM ecosystem, or where timescales do not facilitate the procurement and establishment of an external service integrator. It is also used by organizations that have a business, regulatory or legislative need to retain ownership of the service integration layer.

As part of this structure, the customer may use resource augmentation. This is an approach where many of the individual roles within the service integrator are filled using directly employed internal staff, supplemented by resources provided by an external organization. Even though some of the staff might not be directly employed by the customer, this still fulfils the criteria for an internally sourced service integrator as the customer has overall ownership and control.

Summary: Internally sourced

Suitable for:

- Customers that have in-house service integration capabilities or plan to develop them
- Customers that have business, regulatory or legislative requirements relating to the governance and management of service providers
- Customers that want to retain control and flexibility over the SIAM ecosystem
- Customers whose timescales do not allow procurement of an external service integrator

---

3.2.2 Advantages

The advantages of an internally sourced service integrator include:

- The customer has full control over the service integrator role, with no dependency on an external company, or any of the associated risks and costs.
- Valuable skills remain in-house and there is no loss of key resources or key knowledge.
- The service integrator shares strategic goals with the customer organization, so there is no conflict.
- The service integrator can be flexible and accommodate change without a requirement for any contractual amendments.
- External service providers will not see the service integrator as a competitor and are thus more likely to cooperate and collaborate with the service integrator.
- The service integrator can be established more quickly because it already understands the customer organization's goals and drivers, and because there is no time required to procure and establish an external service integrator.
- The service integrator is part of the same organization that manages service provider contracts, so has direct leverage over service providers, their behavior and performance.

3.2.3 Disadvantages

The disadvantages of an internally sourced service integrator include:

- The customer must develop and maintain the service integrator capability, resources and skills, and design and implement toolsets, sometimes with no experience of SIAM implementation.
- The customer may underestimate the number of resources and the expertise required for the service integrator capability.
- The service integrator is seen as synonymous with the customer organization; this can make it more challenging for them to mediate between the customer and the service providers if there is a conflict.
- The risk that the customer decides to act as the service integrator because they are not fully committed to SIAM, and do not wish to formally establish and outsource the structure. If SIAM is not adopted fully, the benefits will be limited and there will be a further risk that old ways of working continue.
- Internal service providers may not accept the authority of the internal service integrator.

3.3 Hybrid service integrator

In this structure, the customer collaborates with an external organization to take the role of service integrator and provide the service integrator capability.

The service provider roles are performed by external service providers and/or internal service providers.

The hybrid service integrator is exclusively focused on service integration activities and does not take any of the service provider roles.

The hybrid service integrator structure is shown in **figure 11**.

Figure 11: Hybrid service integrator

3.3.1 When does a customer use this structure?

This structure is suitable for organizations that wish to retain an element of involvement in the service integrator role, but do not have sufficient in-house capabilities or resources.

In the hybrid structure, the service integration capability is created through collaboration between the customer and an external service integrator acting as a service integration partner. This can allow the customer organization to learn from an external service integrator that already has expertise in that role.

This structure can be temporary or permanent. If it is temporary, the hybrid approach will end when one of the following has occurred:

- The customer has developed sufficient service integration skills and resources in-house, and has transitioned to an internally sourced structure.
- The customer organization has decided that it no longer wants the hybrid structure, and has transitioned to an external service integrator or a lead supplier structure.

In this structure, it is normal to allocate specific service integration roles, functions and structures to either the customer or the service integration partner. This differentiates this structure from the resource augmentation approach that can be applied to the internally sourced structure.

Summary: Hybrid

Suitable for:

- Customers that want to act as a service integrator but do not have sufficient capability or resources
- Customers that want to learn from an external service integrator
- Customers that want the flexibility of a temporary or permanent hybrid service integrator

---

3.3.2 Advantages

The advantages of a hybrid service integrator include:

- The customer develops skills and resources, and can revert to an internally sourced solution if the service integration partner fails to live up to initial expectations.
- Benefits can be realized more quickly, as the service integrator brings expertise and collaborates with the customer, reducing the time it takes to transition to a SIAM model.
- Access to commercial skills and knowledge: the service integrator can help the customer negotiate with the service providers and avoid common mistakes.

3.3.3 Disadvantages

The disadvantages of a hybrid service integrator include:

- The customer must develop a service integration capability, and recruit and manage resources
- Without clear design, this structure can lead to duplication of skills, missed activities, confusion about responsibilities and poor definition of where the boundaries of operation lie.
- Confusion for the service providers where a clear governance framework and communication plan have not been implemented.
- When the hybrid approach is meant to be temporary, the customer may inadvertently build a long-term dependency on the service integration partner.
- Organizations may adopt the hybrid model because they are reluctant to give up control, not for a valid business reason. This can lead to the benefits of SIAM not being realized.

3.4 Lead supplier as service integrator

In this structure, the role of service integrator is taken by an external organization that is also an external service provider. This can occur when:

- An existing service provider successfully bids to be the service integrator as part of a procurement process
- The existing service integrator successfully bids to be a service provider as part of a procurement process
- One external organization wins two parts of a tender and so becomes the service integrator and a service provider

The organization that is a service provider and the service integrator is referred to as the lead supplier.

This structure is sometimes referred to as 'guardian' or 'custodian'. It is important to emphasize that the contractual relationship in this structure remains between the customer organization and the service providers. The service integrator does not have a contractual relationship with the service providers.

Prime vendor

The lead supplier structure is different from the model known as 'prime' or 'prime vendor', where a service provider subcontracts other service providers to deliver the service and the customer only has a contractual relationship with the prime vendor.

Any of the service providers in any of the four SIAM structures could be a prime vendor, using one or more subcontracted providers as part of its own service delivery. However, these subcontracts are not visible within the SIAM ecosystem. The relationships in the SIAM ecosystem are between the service provider, service integrator and customer. The subcontracts of a particular service provider are not relevant from the SIAM perspective if the service provider can deliver its service to the agreed levels.

Figure 12 shows the lead supplier structure.

Figure 12: Lead supplier as service integrator

3.4.1 When does a customer use this structure?

A customer would choose this structure for the same reasons that it would choose an externally sourced service integrator, i.e. it does not have its own service integration capabilities or resources and does not wish to develop and maintain them.

In this structure, when the customer goes out to tender to choose a service integrator, one of its existing service providers may already have in-depth knowledge of the customer organization, and the customer knows and trusts it. This could facilitate that service provider also acting as the service integrator.

Conversely, the current service integrator may also have expertise in the delivery of one or more of the services (or service elements) and could be selected for that reason.

If a single organization is acting as both the service integrator and a service provider, there are management considerations that need to be addressed. These include:

- Making sure there is no unfair advantage for the service integrator or the service provider
- Maintaining the impartiality of the service integrator role
- Ensuring that the customer is not being charged twice for the same capabilities

This requires clear segregation of duties in the lead supplier, often known as 'Chinese walls'.

The service integrator and service provider roles should be viewed and managed as two separate entities (as if they were separate organizations). They will each have their own contract or agreement, roles, responsibilities and reporting requirements.

Ideally, different resources will work in the service integrator and service provider entities to reduce the likelihood of any conflict of interest.

Summary: Lead supplier

Suitable for:

- Customers that have a trusted service provider that also has service integration capabilities
- Customers that have a trusted service integrator that also has service provider capabilities
- Customers that are prepared for another organization to take the service integrator role
- Customers that do not have service integration capabilities or resources and do not plan to develop them

---

3.4.2 Advantages

The advantages of a lead supplier service integrator are mostly the same as those for an externally sourced service integrator.

There are some additional advantages:

- Where the service integrator is currently acting as a service provider, the set-up process can be faster as there is an existing relationship with the customer.

- From the customer's perspective, the service integrator has a vested interest. If the service fails, it will be subject to penalties at the service provider level, so it has an extra incentive to deliver to agreed targets.

3.4.3 Disadvantages

The disadvantages of a lead supplier service integrator are mostly the same as those for an externally sourced service integrator.

There are some additional disadvantages:

- The organization acting as the service integrator and service provider might not have effective internal governance, leading to knowledge 'leaking' between the two roles. This will create relationship issues between the service integrator and other service providers if this is perceived as an unfair advantage.
- The organization acting as the service integrator and service provider might be perceived to be biased, even if this is not the case, which can also lead to the service integrator/service provider relationships suffering.
- The organization acting as service integrator and service provider might charge the customer twice for the same resources, for example service desk resources shared between the two roles, or management resources shared between the service provider and service integrator roles.
- The service integrator part of the organization could treat its service provider function harshly or unfairly to try to prevent any allegations of bias, which can also create relationship and service management issues.

CHAPTER 4: SIAM AND OTHER PRACTICES

This section of the Body of Knowledge looks at examples of enabling practices, and how they relate to a SIAM ecosystem.

This includes examples from the management frameworks, methods and standards of:

1. Service management (including ITIL, VeriSM™ and ISO standards)
2. COBIT
3. Lean
4. DevOps
5. Agile, including Agile Service Management

For each practice, there is a short summary followed by examples of its relevance to a SIAM ecosystem.

This is not an exhaustive list. There are other practices that can complement and support implementation, operation and improvement in a SIAM ecosystem. These include:

- ADKAR: for organizational change
- BiSL: for business information management
- TOGAF®, IT4IT and other architectural practices
- CMMI: for services, for process assessments
- OBASHI: for mapping relationships, dependencies, and flows of data and information
- Project management methodologies

4.1 Service management

Service management defines the capabilities that support the implementation and management of quality IT services that meet the needs of the business.

Service management is performed by service providers through an appropriate mix of people, process and information technology.

There are two service management practices and several standards that are particularly relevant to SIAM:

1. ITIL
2. VeriSM
3. ISO standards

4.1.1 What is ITIL?

ITIL is the most widely accepted approach to IT service management in the world. ITIL can help individuals and organizations use IT to realize business change, transformation and growth.

ITIL advocates that IT services are aligned to the needs of the business and support its core processes. It provides guidance to organizations and individuals on how to gain optimal value from IT and digital services.

The key elements of ITIL 4 are:

- The four dimensions
- The service value system (SVS), containing the service value chain (SVC), practices and guiding principles

4.1.1.1 ITIL in a SIAM ecosystem

In most cases, transitions to SIAM will take place in an environment that already uses some IT service management processes or elements based on ITIL.

SIAM does not replace ITIL; it builds on service management elements and extends them across the ecosystem where they are relevant to the SIAM model. This might include service management processes, or ITIL concepts, such as the SVS, dimensions, practices and techniques. SIAM adapts them to work effectively in a multi-service provider environment.

While ITIL includes some general guidance for operating in multi-provider ecosystems, it is designed for use in any ecosystem. SIAM, specifically and uniquely, provides in-depth guidance for multi-provider ecosystems, including structural, organizational and functional elements.

4.1.1.2 The service value chain

The ITIL SVS provides a holistic approach to the co-creation of value through service relationships. At the heart of the service value system is the service value chain – a flexible operating model for the creation, delivery and continual improvement of services. The SVC defines six key activities:

- Plan
- Improve
- Engage
- Design and Transition
- Obtain/Build
- Deliver and Support

These activities are interconnected, with each activity receiving and generating triggers for further action. The tasks can be combined in many different sequences, which means the SVC allows an organization to define a number of variants of value streams to react to changing demands from stakeholders effectively and efficiently.

These value streams are equally useful in SIAM, in particular when mapped across service providers to understand better the interactions and cooperation required between them.

4.1.1.3 The four dimensions

A holistic approach to service management is key in ITIL. It defines four dimensions of service management that are critical to the successful facilitation of value for customers and other stakeholders:

- **Organizations and people**: An organization needs a culture that supports its objectives, with the right level of capacity and competency among its workforce
- **Information and technology**: This includes information and knowledge, as well as the technologies required for the management of services
- **Partners and suppliers**: This refers to an organization's relationships with those other businesses that are involved in the design, deployment, delivery, support and continual improvement of services
- **Value streams and processes**: This defines the activities, workflows, controls and procedures to achieve agreed objectives, describing how the various parts of the organization work in an integrated and coordinated way to create value through products and services

SIAM is mentioned specifically in the Partners and Suppliers dimension. However, in order for a SIAM model to meet its objectives, it is important to look at SIAM aspects of the other dimensions (Organizations and People, see **section 7**; Information and Technology, see **section 6.4**; and Value Streams and Processes, see **section 6.2**).

4.1.1.4 The practices

In ITIL, a practice is a set of organizational resources designed for performing work or accomplishing an objective. This includes the service management processes from previous versions of ITIL, but expands the concept. The practices need aspects such as culture, technology, information and data management to be considered to achieve holistic ways of working.

Within a SIAM transformation program, consideration should be given as to how existing ITIL processes and practices need to be adapted to integrate with the local practices of multiple service providers.

For example, the incident management process will follow similar steps, but will need adaptation to support the transfer of incidents and updating of related information between the service providers and the service integrator.

4.1.1.5 The guiding principles

The guiding principles are recommendations that guide an organization in all circumstances. A guiding principle is universal and enduring.

The ITIL guiding principles are:

- Focus on value.
- Start where you are.
- Progress iteratively with feedback.
- Collaborate and promote visibility.
- Think and work holistically.
- Keep it simple and practical.
- Optimize and automate.

They allow professionals to define approaches and navigate difficult decisions and should be followed at every stage of service delivery. ITIL's focus on collaboration, automation and keeping things simple reflect principles found within SIAM good practice.

4.1.2 VeriSM

4.1.2.1 What is VeriSM?

> *"VeriSM is a service management approach for the digital age that considers service management from the organizational level, looking at the end-to-end view rather than focusing on the IT department. The premise is that digital products and services require changes at all levels of the organization including people, technology and ways of working.*
>
> *Based on the VeriSM model (Define, Produce, Provide and Respond), it explains how organizations can adopt a range of management practices in a flexible way to deliver the right product or service at the right time to their consumers."*[14]

VeriSM was created by the International Foundation for Digital Competences (IFDC) in 2017. It is a service management operating model for an organization, which defines several key areas:

- **Governance**: The underpinning system of directing and controlling the activities of an organization.
- **Consumer**: Provides the requirements for products and services, receives products and services, gives feedback and participates in the verify/review/improve activities.
- **Service management principles**: Based on the organizational governing principles, they provide the 'guardrails' for the products and services delivered, addressing areas such as quality and risk.
- **Management mesh**: How an organization combines its resources, environment and emerging technologies with different management practices to create and deliver products and services.
- The Define, Produce, Provide and Respond **stages.**[15]

4.1.2.2 VeriSM in a SIAM ecosystem

Using techniques from VeriSM can help make sense of the technologies and management practices likely to be evident in a SIAM ecosystem. SIAM recognizes the need to allow service providers to use their own approaches and practices and VeriSM supports this.

The management mesh can be used throughout each stage of the SIAM roadmap to create blueprints depicting specific 'resources', 'environment', 'management practices' and 'emerging technologies' for each service. In the Discovery & Strategy stage, mesh blueprints depicting the 'current state' and 'high level requirements' can be created. In the Plan & Build stage, mesh blueprints for the 'full requirements' and 'gaps' can be created to support Implement. Moreover, in Run & Improve, the

---

[14] *VeriSM™ - A Service Management Approach for The Digital Age*, Van Haren Publishing, 2017.

[15] *https://verism.global/*.

updated mesh provides a view of the current environment and a potential baseline for future requirements.

The VeriSM model stages can also be used to support the SIAM roadmap:

- **Define**: Design of a solution (product or service) using agreed requirements. This aligns to the SIAM roadmap stage Discovery & Strategy.
- **Produce**: Creation of the solution (build, test, deploy), ensuring the outcome meets the needs of the consumer. This aligns to the SIAM roadmap stages Plan & Build and Implement.
- **Provide**: The new/changed solution is available for use. This aligns to the SIAM roadmap stage Run & Improve.
- **Respond**: Support the consumer during performance issues, unexpected occurrences, questions or any other requests. This aligns to the SIAM roadmap stage Run & Improve.

4.1.3 ISO standards

The International Organization for Standardization (ISO) is an independent, non-governmental organization, made up of the standards organizations of its member countries. It is the world's largest developer of voluntary international standards.

The standards help businesses increase productivity while minimizing errors and waste. The standards also serve to safeguard consumers of products and services, ensuring that certified products conform to the minimum standards set.

There are many standards – more than 20,000 – but those that are most applicable in a SIAM environment are:

ISO 900x	Quality management family
ISO/IEC 20000	Service management[16]
ISO 22301	Business continuity management
ISO/IEC 2700x	Security techniques (information security management)
ISO/IEC 30105	IT-enabled services – business process outsourcing
ISO 37500	Guidance on outsourcing
ISO/IEC 38500	Governance of IT

---

[16] IEC refers to the International Electrotechnical Commission, a standards organization for all electrical, electronic and related technologies.

ISO 4400x	Collaborative business relationship management

There are many more and it will depend on the organization, its service providers and external requirements to determine which standards need to be integrated into the SIAM model.

What is ISO/IEC 20000?

ISO/IEC 20000 is the first international standard for IT service management. It was developed in 2005.

ISO/IEC 20000 was originally developed to reflect best-practice guidance contained within the ITIL framework, although it supports other IT service management frameworks and approaches equally, including the Microsoft Operations Framework and components of ISACA®'s COBIT framework.[17]

ISO/IEC 20000 is the international standard for service management and requires an organization to have a Service Management System (SMS) that complies with the requirements of the Standard. The SMS defines several areas including:

- Services, organizations and locations in scope
- Service management policies
- Service management capabilities and competencies
- Service management processes
- Governance of processes operated by other parties, including multiple service providers managed by an internal or external service integrator

As most transitions to SIAM will take place in an environment that already uses some service management processes, the Standard can be useful in SIAM ecosystems, either for certification, to demonstrate capability or as guidance.

For instance, a service provider that does not have ISO/IEC 20000 will be able to use the Standard's requirements, and associated guidance, as the basis for the development of the processes and policies it requires for operating in a SIAM environment.

It can also be used as one of the criteria for selecting service providers for a SIAM ecosystem. However, while the Standard provides an independent assessment of the capability and scope of a service provider's service management system and processes, it will not give any indication of its ability to operate in a SIAM ecosystem.

---

[17] For more information, visit: *www.iso.org/standard/70636.html*.

4.2 COBIT

4.2.1 What is COBIT?

> COBIT is a control framework for the governance and management of enterprise IT.[18]
>
> The latest version is COBIT 2019, which is an evolution of the previous version, COBIT 5.

The official guide from ISACA documents nine principles of COBIT, broadly aligned to governance system principles and governance framework principles.

Governance system principles:

- Provide stakeholder value and satisfy stakeholder needs.
- A governance system is built from a number of components that work together in a holistic way.
- A governance system should be dynamic. Each time one or more of the design factors is changed, the impact of these changes should be considered.
- Separating governance from management – clearly distinguish between governance and management activities and structures.
- Tailor and prioritize to the enterprise's needs, using a set of design factors as parameters of governance system components.
- A governance system should focus not only on the IT function but also on all technology and information processing.

Governance framework principles:

- A governance framework should be based on a conceptual model, identifying the key components and relationships among components.
- A governance framework should allow the addition of new content while maintaining integrity and consistency.
- Alignment to relevant major related standards, frameworks and regulations.

It also defines the seven supporting enablers that form the framework:

1. Processes
2. Organizational structures
3. Principles, policies and procedures
4. Information
5. Culture, ethics and behavior
6. People, skills and competencies
7. Services, infrastructure and applications

---

[18] For more information, visit: *www.isaca.org/resources/cobit*.

COBIT includes:

- **A framework to organize IT governance objectives and practices**: Organizes IT governance objectives and good practices by IT domains and processes, and links them to business requirements.
- **Process descriptions**: A reference process model and common language for everyone in an organization. The processes map to responsibility areas of plan, build, run and monitor.
- **Control objectives**: Provide a complete set of high-level requirements to be considered by management for effective control of each IT process.
- **Management guidelines**: Help assign responsibility, agree on objectives, measure performance and illustrate interrelationship with other processes.
- **Maturity models**: Assess maturity and capability per process and help address gaps.
- **Performance management**: Refers to how well an organization's governance and management system, plus all the components, work.

4.2.2 COBIT in a SIAM ecosystem

The nine principles of COBIT and the seven supporting enablers have clear synergies with SIAM as described in **sections 2**, **6** and **7**, and the **SIAM Process Guides**.

Table 1 shows how the COBIT components can map to SIAM.

Table 1: COBIT Components and SIAM Components

COBIT component	SIAM component
Framework	Practices, governance model and structural elements
Process descriptions	Process models and processes
Management guidelines	Governance model
Maturity model	No direct equivalent
Performance management	Performance management and reporting framework

In a SIAM ecosystem, governance and management of information become more complex owing to the number of stakeholders and organizations involved. The control objectives and maturity models from COBIT can be particularly useful in addressing this complexity during the Discovery & Strategy and Plan & Build stages of the SIAM roadmap.

An enterprise governance model like COBIT can help to deliver outcomes including:

1. **Benefits realization**: This consists of creating value for the enterprise, maintaining and increasing value derived from existing investments, and eliminating IT initiatives and assets that are not

creating enough value. The basic principles are delivery of fit-for-purpose services and solutions, on time and within budget initiatives.

2. **Resource optimization**: This ensures that appropriate capabilities are in place to execute the strategic plan and that sufficient, appropriate and effective resources are provided. Resource optimization ensures that an integrated, economical IT infrastructure is provided, new technology is introduced as required by the business and obsolete systems are updated or replaced.

4.3 Lean

4.3.1 What is Lean?

The core idea of Lean is to maximize customer value while minimizing waste. Simply, Lean means creating more value for customers with fewer resources.

A Lean organization understands customer value and focuses its key processes to continuously increase it. The goal is to provide optimal value to the customer through an optimal value creation process that has zero waste.[19]

Lean thinking started in Toyota as a way to improve the speed of the products and services moving through an organization's processes by constantly improving flow and quality to optimize the level of customer value and satisfaction. The Lean approach includes five principles:

- Specify **value**, as defined by the customer
- Identify the **value stream**
- Create an even **flow** of value-adding activities
- Let the customer **pull** the product or service through the value stream
- Strive for **perfection** through continuous improvement

Lean techniques focus on removing or minimizing any activities that do not add value to the finished product. These activities are referred to as 'Muda' (waste). Waste types were defined by Toyota first and have since been 'translated' to a service-related context. The waste types are described in **table 2**.

Table 2: Lean Waste Types

Traditional waste types	Examples of waste type in service context
Transport	- Moving tickets between operators - Moving devices around and out to users
Inventory	- Queues of tickets, alerts, requests - Lots of devices, PCs or service requests

---

[19] Lean Enterprise Institute, for more information visit: *www.lean.org/*.

Motion	• Flipping through many screens or fields to complete an activity • Having to put in the same information multiple times to complete an activity • Looking for necessary information • Switching between different tasks
Waiting	• The time a ticket or product sits idle, waiting for action • A user waiting for the service desk on the phone or at the service desk counter
Over-processing	• Double handling • Too many approvals and controls • Controls being performed before things are done • Constraints on the process flow due to bottlenecks, inflexibilities and decisions not being timely
Over-production	• Delivering before the agreed time • Delivering more service than agreed • Preparing things ahead of time
Defects	• Mistakes, misunderstandings, incomplete or wrong information on a ticket
Unused skills or talent	• Too little autonomy and responsibility given to employees • Skilled employees working on simple tasks • Employees working on tasks they do not have the required skills or knowledge for

In addition to being a way to improve processes or value streams, Lean affects the entire organizational culture, involving and affecting everyone. Lean thinking has been applied to other sectors, including IT service management. For example, Lean IT takes Lean manufacturing principles and applies them to the development and management of IT products and services.

The Lean culture and way of thinking can be said to be the foundation of both Agile and DevOps ways of working.

4.3.2 Lean in a SIAM ecosystem

Using Lean techniques can help to increase delivered value and maximize efficiencies in a SIAM ecosystem.

The application of Lean could be relevant in all stages of the SIAM roadmap:

- **Discovery & Strategy**: When establishing a SIAM project, mapping and understanding the current state of the organization could be done using Lean approaches and tools.

- **Plan & Build**: When defining the collaboration model, it could be useful to include Lean principles of continuous improvement, emphasizing the prevention of errors over reactive fixes.
- **Implement**: Applying Lean to this stage could in many cases increase throughput and speed.
- **Run & Improve**: The Lean principles and underlying culture of continuous improvement could form the general approach for improvement across the ecosystem.

Lean techniques can also deliver value when applied to processes. Every step in every process should be analyzed. Considerations should include:

- What value does this step add to the outputs from the previous step?
- Does that value contribute to the expected outputs from the whole process?
- Does this step repeat any work done in a previous step?
- Does this step repeat any work done in any other process?
- Are there any times during the step when no work is being carried out?
- Can the process step cope with the expected workload?

One of the key concepts from Lean is that quality should be designed into a product, not added into it by inspection. Wherever possible, processes should be designed to consistently deliver outputs with the required quality. Any subsequent quality inspections by the service integrator or customer should be examined to justify why they are required.

For example, consider the management of a change request sent from a service provider to the service integrator for approval, as shown in **table 3**.

Table 3: Management of a Change Request and Sources of Waste

Process step	Potential waste
Send change request to the service integrator	• Defect: the change request does not hold the correct – or adequate – information
Service integrator logs and reviews the change request	• Waiting: the change request sits in an email inbox until read • Over-processing: the change request has already been reviewed by the service provider
Service integrator's change manager assesses the change	• Waiting: the change request sits in an email inbox until read • Over-processing: the change request has already been assessed by the service provider
Change manager circulates the change request to the integrated change advisory board members	• Waiting: the change manager only sends out change requests once a week

Integrated change advisory board members assess the change	• Waiting: the change request sits in an email inbox until read • Over-processing: some board members do not have the skills or knowledge to assess the change
Integrated change advisory board schedules the change	• Waiting: the board only meets once a week
Change manager authorizes deployment of the change	• Waiting: the change manager does not authorize until the day after the Integrated change advisory board meeting

4.4 DevOps

4.4.1 What is DevOps?

"DevOps represents a change in IT culture, focusing on rapid IT service delivery through the adoption of Agile, Lean practices in the context of a system-oriented approach. DevOps emphasizes people (and culture), and it seeks to improve collaboration between operations and development teams. DevOps implementations utilize technology – especially automation tools that can leverage an increasingly programmable and dynamic infrastructure from a life cycle perspective."[20]

DevOps embraces the full lifecycle of software development and operation. It is a flexible and evolving philosophy and approach, not a standard or a framework with prescriptive processes. It focuses on bringing an organization's development and operations capabilities together into cross-functional, autonomous teams with shared responsibilities.

DevOps thinking focuses on aspects including:

1. Ownership and accountability
2. Systems thinking
3. Continual experimentation and learning
4. Collaborative culture and sharing
5. Automation
6. Elimination of waste/Lean principles
7. Measurement

DevOps values are described as CALMS and are shown in **table 4**.

---

[20] Gartner, *www.gartner.com/en/information-technology/glossary/devops*.

Table 4: DevOps CALMS Values

Culture	The DevOps scope can be thought of as people, process and technology. Culture addresses the people and process aspects. Culture includes communication, collaboration and behaviors.
Automation	Automation includes tools that enable the automation of tasks like testing and deploying software. Release management, configuration management and monitoring and control tools all enable automation.
Lean	Lean refers to creating more value for customers with fewer resources. See **section 4.3.1**.
Measurement	From a DevOps perspective, measurement is essential. Measurement will demonstrate the value of DevOps, and also provide feedback on the products and services being developed. This feedback is used to highlight improvement opportunities.
Sharing	Sharing improves communication and collaboration and provides opportunities for the organization to learn and improve. Sharing can be thought of as a feedback loop.

4.4.2 DevOps in a SIAM ecosystem

DevOps and SIAM approaches can initially seem to be in conflict with each other. DevOps focuses on end-to-end ownership of products and services, with autonomous, self-managing teams. SIAM ecosystems often break services down and allocate management responsibility for different elements to different service providers.

However, the two share a common goal – delivering high-quality products and services that lead to customer satisfaction – and the DevOps CALMS values can be used to help adapt DevOps for a SIAM ecosystem as shown in **table 5**.

Table 5: DevOps CALMS values in a SIAM ecosystem

Culture	In a SIAM ecosystem, the logical team that is responsible for a product or service might include personnel from multiple service providers. Instilling a DevOps culture would include encouraging a sense of collective ownership and building strong relationships across the team.
Automation	Automation can be more challenging where there are multiple service providers, possibly using different toolsets. Automation needs to be considered when developing the SIAM tooling strategy, and there could be a forum that meets to discuss further opportunities for automation.

Lean	The number of service providers involved in a SIAM ecosystem can unintentionally create waste, when information needs to be passed between service providers and tasks are duplicated. A Lean focus helps to minimize waste. DevOps seeks to reduce hand-offs between teams; SIAM needs to have clarity of where hand-offs are taking place.
Measurement	Both DevOps and SIAM see measurement as essential to show value is being delivered and efficiencies are being realized. DevOps teams can support measurement automation, and the service integrator can help to create end-to-end measurement across the ecosystem.
Sharing	DevOps teams may only need to share information within the team, or within one organization. In a SIAM ecosystem, the service integrator needs to build a culture that encourages and rewards sharing between service providers.

4.4.2.1 Ownership and accountability

DevOps is designed to deliver working software and solutions at pace, with a culture of full ownership and empowerment of the DevOps team(s). This can seem at odds with the governance and assurance roles of the service integrator, and it can cause tension with service providers that have adopted DevOps, as the service integrator can be considered to add delay to the implementation of change, with no added value.

DevOps uses the same team to specify, develop, test, deploy, and fully support services, including applications and infrastructure. This can conflict with the segregation of duties required in some SIAM governance models (often defined in sourcing contracts).

DevOps thinking can also conflict with SIAM sourcing approaches and grouping of services, where different service providers support infrastructure and applications. Most DevOps teams prefer to be responsible for all aspects of the service. The SIAM model needs to balance the benefits that DevOps ways of working can deliver with the complexity of the sourcing environment.

4.4.2.2 Systems thinking

Systems thinking emphasizes the performance of the entire system, rather than focusing on a single silo, team or department. It focuses on all the business value streams enabled by IT. In high-performing organizations, flows are visible, for example as process or value stream maps. People self-organize to improve flow.

In a DevOps environment, systems thinking is focused on understanding the flow of work from Dev to Ops and ways to increase flow. In a SIAM ecosystem, the focus is on the flow of work between and across service providers, highlighting and addressing any issues or bottlenecks.

4.4.2.3 Continual experimentation and learning

An important DevOps concept is the incremental deployment of new functionality, followed by user feedback before the next increment. This can be problematic in a SIAM ecosystem, as the deployment will impact multiple service providers.

If DevOps is adopted, the service providers and the service integrator will need to collaborate to build and maintain comprehensive automated test suites for the end-to-end services.

DevOps also encourages a culture of experimentation and learning in ways of working. Failures are a learning opportunity, not a blaming opportunity. This culture can be used to reinforce a culture of collaboration in a SIAM ecosystem.

4.4.2.4 Collaborative culture and sharing

DevOps behavioral concepts can be particularly useful in building a strong culture in SIAM ecosystems.

The focus on culture and sharing encourages collaboration and communication throughout the life of a product or service, using co-located multi-disciplinary teams that all share the goal of delivering outcomes that the customer wants.

For example, in a DevOps environment all members of the team are accountable for the success of a change; they take collective responsibility and accountability for approval. Contrast that with an approach that expects a single individual to be accountable. Using collective accountability for decisions in SIAM ecosystems can help to create a collaborative culture.

4.4.2.5 Automation

Automation of activities such as testing and deployment is an important element of DevOps. Automation can speed up delivery and reduce risks. Automation needs to be integrated with the change management governance requirements in a SIAM ecosystem.

DevOps thinking can also help to address some common SIAM challenges, applying automation to overcome problems caused by a lack of integrated toolsets.

4.4.2.6 Elimination of waste/Lean principles

The end-to-end ownership of products and services advocated by DevOps thinking ("you build it, you run it") reduces hand-offs between teams. This allows greater clarity about the value streams associated with a product or service and makes it simpler to identify where there are wasteful activities, because fewer people are involved.

In a SIAM environment, the challenge is to balance the value that comes from the end-to-end view of a service against the complexity created by having multiple service providers involved in the delivery. Hand-offs between service providers need to be carefully reviewed to analyze where duplicated or redundant activities can be removed, and how to involve the service integrator.

4.4.2.7 Measurement

DevOps prioritizes getting feedback about products and services quickly, using techniques like short feedback loops and Agile development practices. Feedback is used to identify improvement opportunities related to products and services and to ways of working.

In a SIAM model, the service integrator must ensure that measurement takes place across the ecosystem for end-to-end service delivery. Measuring each service provider individually does not provide a complete picture. DevOps thinking can also be applied to help identify ways of automating measurement, reducing the management overhead related to collecting and sharing data.

4.5 Agile, including Agile Service Management

4.5.1 agile, Agile and agility

The word 'agile' is an adjective and means *"able to move quickly and easily; able to think quickly, solve problems, and have new ideas"*.[21] Being agile refers to a mindset or organizational culture (how we see ourselves and behave, and what we value). Building an agile culture offers a way to harness the power of people in an organization, and to find ways to be more adaptive, innovative and resilient in a fast-paced world.

'Agile' (with a capital A) is also used to refer to a group of frameworks and methods used for the development and management of projects or initiatives. Examples of Agile methods and frameworks are Scrum, Kanban, eXtreme programming and Dynamic Systems Development Method (DSDM).

The word 'agility' is generally used in the context of enterprise or organizational agility. In broad terms, it means the ability to adapt easily to change. Through organizational agility, companies strive to improve speed of execution, and the ability to better respond and adapt to customer needs, and engage and empower employees.

In many publications, 'agile' and 'Agile' may be used interchangeably, but it is important to understand the underlying difference between the two words.

4.5.2 What is Agile?

> *"Agile is a set of values and principles under which requirements and solutions evolve through the collaborative effort of self-organizing cross-functional teams."*[22]

Agile thinking originated in software development. It used and built on Lean techniques from the manufacturing sector. In 2001, the Agile Manifesto was published, which encapsulates the 4 values and 12 guiding principles for Agile.

Agile thinking and the Manifesto have been successfully applied in many different disciplines and situations, including project management, change management, service management, DevOps and SIAM.

Compared to traditional 'waterfall' approaches, Agile delivers changes more frequently, with smaller amounts of change delivered in each iteration and/or increment. This provides a faster realization of benefits and value, and reduced business risk.

The Agile approach also allows easier change of direction. For example, allowing a business to realize that a new service will not deliver the expected benefits before too much investment is made in its development.

---

[21] *www.itsmacademy.com/content/WhatIsASM.pdf*.

[22] Wikipedia, *https://en.wikipedia.org/wiki/Agile_software_development*.

4.5.3 What is Agile Service Management?

> *"Agile Service Management (Agile SM) ensures that ITSM processes reflect Agile values and are designed with "just enough" control and structure in order to effectively and efficiently deliver services that facilitate customer outcomes when and how they are needed."[23]*

The goals of Agile SM include:

- Ensuring that Agile values and principles are embedded in every service management process from design through to implementation and continual improvement
- Improving IT's entire ability to meet customer requirements faster
- Being effective and efficient (Lean)
- Designing processes with "just enough" scalable control and structure
- Providing services that deliver ongoing customer value

4.5.4 Agile in a SIAM ecosystem

Any SIAM implementation will benefit from a focus on the values and principles of Agile.

The values from the Agile Manifesto can be adapted to apply in SIAM ecosystems; all parties in the ecosystem should value:

- Individuals and interactions over processes and tools
- Working services over comprehensive documentation
- Collaboration over contracts
- Responding to change over following a plan

According to the Agile Manifesto, there is value in the items mentioned second, but more in those mentioned first. For example, the first value indicates that the best way to improve performance is to focus on human aspects, i.e. more emphasis on individuals and interaction, rather than focusing on processes and tools.

Agile approaches can be used to design, develop and implement many parts of a SIAM model, SIAM structure and SIAM roadmap, including:

- Processes
- Policies
- Tooling
- Service improvements
- Structural elements

---

[23] *The Agile Service Management Guide, https://devopsinstitute.com/ebook-agile-service-management-guide/.*

Scrum is one of the Agile methods commonly adopted by organizations. It includes the concept of a sprint retrospective, which can be used in a SIAM ecosystem as a structural element. A sprint retrospective is an opportunity for the team to review and create an improvement plan for the next sprint (or iteration).

A typical sprint retrospective covers:

- What worked well and what should we continue doing?
- What could be improved and what should we stop doing?
- What will we commit to and start doing in the next sprint?

Applying the 4 values and 12 guiding principles from the Agile Manifesto to IT service management and SIAM can:

- Improve delivery and the flow of work
- Improve customer satisfaction
- Support collaboration across the SIAM ecosystem
- Support incremental process improvement
- Provide flexibility
- Allow early identification of course corrections or changes of direction

Table 6 provides some adapted examples of the 12 Agile principles, applied in a SIAM ecosystem.

Table 6: Examples of Agile Principles Applied in a SIAM Ecosystem

Agile principle	SIAM application
The highest priority is to satisfy the customer through early and continuous delivery	Agile could be applied in a phased implementation of the SIAM ecosystem to provide a quicker result with incremental learning.
Deliver releases frequently	The end-to-end change and release management processes and supporting governance should be designed to support the required rate of test, approval and deployment of releases.
Build projects around motivated individuals, and trust them to get the job done	The service integrator should trust the service providers and empower them to deliver their services without – or with minimum – interference (and vice versa).
Face-to-face conversation is the most efficient and effective method of conveying information	Working groups and process forums are an effective way to convey important information to service providers. Video conferencing and chat

	technology can be used to make this virtually 'face to face'.
Continuous attention to excellence and good design enhances agility	Process forums can support the development and use of best practice across the service provider community.
Simplicity is essential	The SIAM model should be understandable. If not, service providers may have difficulty in understanding and applying it.
The best outputs emerge from self-organizing teams	Embodied in a SIAM environment through trust, empowerment, working groups and process forums.
Reflect at regular intervals on how to become more effective, then tune and adjust behaviors	Process forums and governance boards should use data and information to identify areas for improvement, then action those improvements. Positive behaviors should be encouraged and rewarded.

4.5.5 Agile Service Management in a SIAM ecosystem

Agile Service Management in a SIAM ecosystem can enable:

- **Agile process design**: Uses Agile methods to design IT service management processes. These are designed and implemented in small, frequent releases, typically using two to four-week cycles. The first cycle should deliver a minimum viable process (MVP), which is the smallest amount of functionality that is needed. This enables early use and feedback, which is then fed into the next cycle.

- **Agile process improvement**: Uses Agile methods to improve processes. Within one service provider, the process owner should be empowered to improve the process. In the wider SIAM ecosystem, the process forum should be awarded that empowerment. Individual improvements should be designed and implemented using a regular, short cycle. The priority should be customer satisfaction. Lean thinking can be applied to find and remove waste and activities that add no value.

Summary

These, and other, practices can provide support to SIAM. Care should be taken to understand them in more detail, and to adapt them where required for use in a SIAM ecosystem.

CHAPTER 5: SIAM ROLES AND RESPONSIBILITIES

This section of the BoK looks at roles and responsibilities in a typical SIAM ecosystem. This includes looking at the specific role of each SIAM layer, and the way that roles are grouped into structural elements.

> A role is defined as "*the position or purpose that someone or something has in a situation, organization, society, or relationship*".[24]
>
> A responsibility is defined as "*something that it is your job or duty to deal with*".[25]

5.1 Roles and the SIAM roadmap

Within a SIAM ecosystem, roles and responsibilities need to be defined, allocated, monitored and improved.

Principles and policies for roles and responsibilities are defined during the Discovery & Strategy stage of the SIAM roadmap, before detail is added during Plan & Build. Roles and responsibilities are then allocated during the Implement stage and monitored during Run & Improve.

The four main activities related to roles and responsibilities are:

1. Definition of principles and policies
2. Design
3. Allocation
4. Monitoring and improvement

5.1.1 Definition of principles and policies

Definition of the principles and policies for roles and responsibilities is a vital step in the design of the SIAM ecosystem.

During the Discovery & Strategy stage, existing roles and job descriptions are mapped and compared to required responsibilities (for instance, those defined within the governance framework) and the selected SIAM structure.

During the Discovery & Strategy stage, the roles and responsibilities themselves are not detailed; they are revisited and more detail is added during the design activities in the Plan & Build stage.

There is no single, ideal mapping of roles and responsibilities for a SIAM ecosystem. Each SIAM model will be different, depending on what the customer organization wishes to retain, and what it is prepared to source externally from the service integrator and/or the service providers.

---

[24] *https://dictionary.cambridge.org/dictionary/english/role*.

[25] *https://dictionary.cambridge.org/dictionary/english/responsibility*.

The customer organization's decision about what to source internally, and what to source externally, will be influenced by several factors:

- The overall objectives for implementing SIAM
- The selected SIAM structure
- The customer's strategy and organizational goals
- Customer capability and skill levels
- What the customer regards as a strategic capability that is essential to retain
- Existing service provider relationships and outsourced roles and responsibilities

---

The service 'menu'

We can think of this process as like choosing food from a menu. The customer is given the opportunity to review the roles and responsibilities and can select the options that are attractive to it.

This process puts the customer in control, allowing it to retain activities it sees as too risky or complex to outsource, and to transfer responsibility for tasks that it no longer wishes to undertake itself, or that can be effectively sourced externally.

5.1.2 Design

During the Plan & Build roadmap stage, detailed roles and responsibilities are designed using the outline SIAM model and outline process models, the SIAM structure and the governance framework.

5.1.3 Allocation

During the Implement stage, roles and responsibilities are allocated.

There are some roles that will always be allocated to specific SIAM layers:

- The customer organization must retain any roles that are mandated by legislation or regulations.
- The service integrator will always be accountable for service governance, management, integration, assurance and coordination, including end-to-end service management, service provider management, monitoring and reporting.
- The service providers will fulfil service delivery roles.

5.1.4 Monitoring and improvement

Once the roles and responsibilities are established, they are monitored to determine their effectiveness and to identify any opportunities for improvement. Improvements can be made to the individual roles and to the interfaces between roles.

Roles will need to be reviewed following any restructuring activities across the organization to ensure they remain aligned and effective.

5.2 How is a role different in a SIAM ecosystem?

The definition of roles and responsibilities in a SIAM ecosystem must recognize that they will be applied in a multi-provider environment. Without careful design and management of roles and responsibilities, there is a higher risk that activities could be missed or duplicated as more parties are involved and the ecosystem is more complex.

Mapping activities

In a SIAM ecosystem, one process or activity might span the three layers. For example, consider change management:

- **Customer layer:** has input to change authorization and scheduling
- **Service integrator layer:** manages the integrated change management process
- **Service provider:** initiates changes, presents them to the change advisory board, implements changes

There is also an opportunity for multiple roles to be performed by one person. For example, a process manager for a service provider might have:

- A change management role, attending the change advisory board
- A problem management role, attending a problem management working group
- A knowledge management role, providing input into knowledge articles

The way that roles are allocated will depend on factors including the size and complexity of the SIAM ecosystem and resource availability and capability.

5.2.1 The role of the customer organization

Outside of a SIAM model, it is usual for the customer to have a direct relationship with its service providers. In the SIAM ecosystem, the customer needs to understand that its role is to support and empower the service integrator. If the customer continues to work directly with service providers within a SIAM ecosystem, it may inadvertently create a 'Shadow IT' structure.

5.2.2 The role of retained capabilities

For staff who are part of the retained capabilities, adapting to SIAM means relinquishing direct control of service providers and stepping back from day-to-day management of service provision. Their role needs to be strategic and proactive, rather than operational and reactive.

The retained capabilities role needs to have a strong relationship with the service integrator. Its purpose is to provide direction, and enable service integrator autonomy without creating a dictatorship.

The customer owns the contracts with the service providers, but the service integrator is managing delivery against them. The retained capabilities need to let the service integrator carry out its role without undermining it.

5.2.3 The role of the service integrator

The role of the service integrator involves being the agent of the customer, acting on its behalf. This means doing the right thing for the customer, while not undermining its own organizational goals and objectives.

The service integrator also represents the service providers and the end-to-end service to the customer organization.

The service integrator role relies on good relationships. To be effective, it must have a good relationship with the customer organization and the service providers.

The service integrator's role is to assure and facilitate service delivery. It needs to be contractually and commercially aware to carry out its role effectively in the SIAM ecosystem. The service integrator needs to focus on service integration and collaboration across multiple service providers.

5.2.4 The role of service providers

Working collaboratively can be a new approach and a culture change for service providers. They need to adapt to working with potential competitors, and adjust to having a relationship with the service integrator rather than their customer.

They may have to change their ways of working and their structure to be effective in the SIAM ecosystem. Their role will require a focus on service objectives, balancing them against their own organizational objectives.

5.3 Role description: Customer organization, including retained capabilities

Description	The customer's role within the SIAM ecosystem is that of the commissioning organization. It also includes the retained capabilities that carry out corporate governance of the SIAM ecosystem.
Typical accountabilities	• Strategic direction • Enterprise architecture • Policy and standards management • Procurement • Contract management • Demand management • Financial and commercial management • Service portfolio management • Corporate risk management • Governance, including governance of the service integrator • Accountability for program and project management
Typical roles	• Head of IT • Head of service • Service owner(s) • Enterprise architect

	• Service architect • Chief finance officer (CFO) • Chief information officer (CIO) • Chief security officer (CSO)
Typical responsibilities	• Defines and assures a core set of policies, standards, procedures and guidelines including architectural, informational, commercial, financial, security and enterprise service architecture. • Develops and owns the IT strategy and strategy for SIAM that align with and support the business strategy. • Develops and owns enterprise architecture, defines the technology, data and application roadmap, and defines the service scope for SIAM. • Provides overarching program and commercial management. • Assures and governs the service integrator. • Manages the service provider relationships at an executive/commercial level. • Overall management of risk. • Resolves contractual disputes. • Owns business relationships and acts as an "intelligent customer" function. • Defines end-to-end service budget.

5.4 Role description: Service integrator

Description	The service integrator layer of the SIAM model is where end-to-end service governance, integration, assurance and coordination are performed.
Typical accountabilities	• End-to-end service management • End-to-end performance management • End-to-end service reporting • Service governance and assurance • Tracking value for money • Continual service improvement
Typical roles	• Head of service integration • Service delivery manager(s) • Service manager(s) • Process owner(s) • Process manager(s) • Service assurance manager(s) • Performance manager(s) • Security manager(s)

Typical responsibilities	• Responsible for end-to-end service management across the service providers and the interface into the customer organization. • Managing service provider relationships at an operational level. • Acting as the customer's "agent" and providing a communication path to the service providers. • Managing end-to-end performance management of all service providers. • Managing performance management of individual service providers against agreed targets. • Coordination of the service providers. • Assuring service provider performance and service delivery. • Governing the service providers, as delegated by the customer organization. • Facilitating process forums. • Managing operational supply and demand for services and capacity. • Consolidated service reporting. • Providing service communications. • Potential responsibility for provision and management of an integrated service management toolset. • Managing the performance of service providers against contractual and service targets.

5.5 Role description: Service provider

Description	Within a SIAM ecosystem, there are multiple service providers. Each service provider is responsible for the delivery of one or more services, or service elements, to the customer. It is responsible for managing the products and technology used to deliver its contracted or agreed services. The service providers can be part of the customer organization or external to it.
Typical accountabilities	• Delivering services required by the customer to defined and agreed standards, policies and architecture • Exhibiting required behaviors for cooperation, collaboration, improvement and innovation • Ensuring cross-service provider service management processes are followed • Working collaboratively with suppliers and the service integrator to resolve issues, incidents and problems, identify improvement opportunities and meet customer outcomes
Typical roles	• Service manager(s) • Account manager(s) • Process owner(s)

	<ul><li>Process manager(s)</li><li>Technical staff</li><li>Service management staff</li></ul>
Typical responsibilities	<ul><li>The delivery of technology and products to deliver services, at agreed service levels and cost.</li><li>Integrating internal service management processes with the end-to-end service management processes.</li><li>Adhering to policies, standards and procedures defined by the customer.</li><li>Adhering to architectural design standards.</li><li>Working collaboratively with the service integrator and other service providers.</li><li>Taking part in structural elements, including process forums.</li></ul>

5.6 Governance roles

Governance is a term that is widely used and often misunderstood. In a SIAM ecosystem, governance refers to the definition and application of policies and standards. These define and ensure the required levels of authority, decision-making and accountability.

COBIT includes three activities in its definition of governance: evaluate, direct and monitor. Lower-level activities (plan, build, etc.) are part of management (see **section 4.2.1**).

This is shown in **figure 13**.

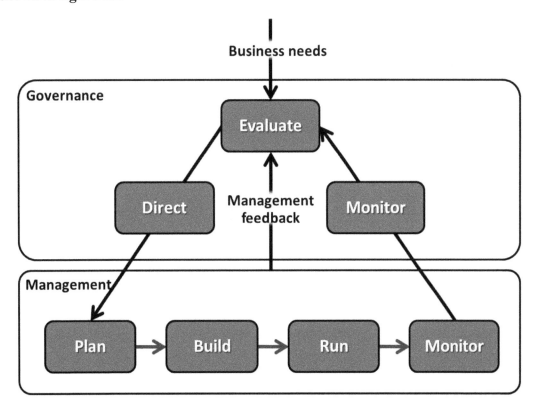

Figure 13: The COBIT® 5 Business Framework for the Governance and Management of Enterprise IT©, 2012, ISACA

The SIAM roles can be mapped onto this model, as shown in **figure 14**.

Figure 14: Mapping SIAM roles onto the COBIT® 5 Business Framework

Governance activities are carried out at strategic, tactical and operational levels through governance boards. These boards form structural elements in the SIAM layers.

Boards are decision-making bodies that are accountable for their outcomes.

The boards discussed in this book provide the required level of governance in a SIAM environment. In complex environments with many different service providers, more boards might be created to address specific areas, for example:

- Information security advisory board
- IT service continuity governance board
- Program board

The board structure that is put in place in a SIAM model needs to balance the level of overhead created by the board meetings against the governance requirements and the outcomes achieved.

5.6.1 Strategic governance: Executive boards

Executive boards provide governance and oversight at the most senior level. These boards also play an important role in establishing a SIAM culture, by demonstrating good behaviors at the most senior levels (see **section 7**).

The attendees for these boards are senior staff with accountability for their organization's role in the SIAM model.

In addition to the executive board attended by all service providers, each service provider has an individual executive board with the customer and the service integrator. This allows a service provider to discuss commercial performance and sensitive issues.

5.6.1.1 Typical attendees

Typical attendees include:

- **Customer:** chief information officer (CIO), chief technology officer (CTO), head of delivery or service delivery director
- **Service integrator:** operations director, contract and commercial director
- **Service providers:** operations director, contract and commercial director, account executive, CIO, CTO

5.6.1.2 Typical frequency

Executive boards are typically held quarterly.

5.6.1.3 Typical agenda

An executive board agenda could include:

- Customer strategy: for the next six months, one year and three years
- Service integrator strategy updates, including any possible clashes or synergy, and opportunities for mutual benefit
- Service provider strategy updates, where appropriate, including any possible clashes or synergy, and opportunities for mutual benefit
- A high-level review of the previous quarter, including successes and issues
- Contractual performance, including any obligations not being met; these are typically discussed at the individual executive boards, unless there is a common issue across all service providers
- Planning for innovation, considering any new items from the service providers/service integrator
- Any other relevant topics

5.6.1.4 Typical inputs

Executive board inputs could include:

- Quarterly and monthly performance information
- Customer and service satisfaction information
- Customer strategy
- Strategic service improvements
- Strategic innovations
- Service integrator and service provider strategies, where relevant
- Service provider technology roadmap

5.6.1.5 Typical outputs

Executive board outputs could include:

- Action and decision logs
- Strategic course corrections or direction changes
- Business change requirements
- Strategic change schedule
- Celebration and communication of success

5.6.2 Tactical board

The tactical board sits between the strategic and operational boards. It forms part of the preparation for the operational board and can be used to carry out discussions before meeting with the customer, for example if a major incident has occurred. It can also be used to identify items for escalation to the strategic board, and acts as a point of escalation for operational boards.

This board is not attended by the customer.

5.6.2.1 Typical attendees

Tactical board attendees are staff from the service integrator and the service providers. The roles present could include:

- Service delivery managers
- Service managers
- Process owners, as required
- Account managers

5.6.2.2 Typical frequency

Tactical boards are typically monthly.

5.6.2.3 Typical agenda

This board is used to discuss service performance and continual improvement, so the agenda will vary depending on any issues that are being experienced.

The service integrator is empowered to interpret the contract on behalf of the customer, so decisions might be made at this meeting about financial or non-financial remediation, which can then be communicated at the operational board.

This board will take direction from the strategic board and use it to create tactical action plans. It will also review changes escalated from the operational boards.

This board will include coordination, mediation, decision-making, assurance and governance.

5.6.2.4 Typical inputs

Tactical board inputs could include:

- Performance data, including customer satisfaction
- Service improvements
- Service provider data

5.6.2.5 Typical outputs

Tactical board outputs could include:

- Action and decision logs
- Tactical change schedule
- Improvement opportunities

5.6.3 Operational boards

The main operational board convenes to discuss service performance at a lower level than the executive and tactical boards.

It will review service performance and acts as an escalation point for all other operational boards and process forums. For example, it may authorize budget or resources to carry out improvement activities identified in a process forum that exceed the approval limit of the process forum attendees.

Other operational boards will be scheduled as required to support decision-making; the most common example of this is the integrated change advisory board.

5.6.3.1 Typical attendees

Operational board attendees could include:

- Customer retained capabilities, where required
- Service integrator
- Service providers
- User representatives
- Process owners
- Process managers
- Service managers

5.6.3.2 Typical frequency

Operational boards are typically monthly.

5.6.3.3 Typical agenda

An operational board agenda could include:

- Review of monthly performance reports, including customer satisfaction
- Actions and decisions
- Critical and major incident reviews
- Escalations from other operational boards and process forums
- Six-monthly compliance and certification policies and procedures review

5.6.3.4 Typical inputs

Operational board inputs could include:

- Monthly reports
- Process reports, for example incident reports
- Improvement plans
- Escalations from other operational board
- Decisions from the tactical and strategic boards

5.6.3.5 Typical outputs

Operational board inputs could include:

- Decision and action logs
- Items for escalation
- Improvement actions

5.6.4 Operational board: Integrated change advisory board

The integrated change advisory board is an operational governance board. It meets this definition because it makes decisions and is held accountable for them. It is chaired and managed by the service integrator.

This board reviews all changes within the scope of its authority that could affect the end-to-end service, regardless of which service provider will implement the change. It focuses on changes that affect multiple service providers, associated risks and unintended impacts on the customer.

The board is also responsible for defining change policy. The policy defines the responsibilities for review and approval of different types of change. This includes the definition of standard or self-contained changes that can be approved locally by a service provider.

Where necessary, changes are escalated to the tactical or strategic boards. 'Review' of changes can encompass any action from detailed investigation through to definition of standard changes that gain automatic approval, or approval of systems for automated test and release (see **section 4.4**). The board seeks to facilitate, not prevent change.

The responsibilities of the integrated change advisory board include:

- Ensuring that all service providers and the customer are aware of relevant changes
- Confirming that:
  - Changes have been evaluated for risk and unintended impact
  - Remediation plans have been verified
  - Appropriate resources have been allocated and made available to implement the change
  - There are robust communication plans in place
  - Ecosystem technical and architectural standards have been met
- Collective approval or otherwise of the change
- Creating mechanisms for standard changes and their automatic approval
- Reviewing completed changes

5.6.4.1 Typical attendees

Integrated change advisory board attendees could include:

- Service integrator change manager (chair)
- Service provider change managers
- Subject matter experts as required
- Customer representation as required

5.6.4.2 Typical frequency

The frequency of the integrated change advisory board varies, relating to the number and scale of changes. Additional emergency meetings can be convened as required.

5.6.4.3 Typical agenda

An integrated change advisory board agenda could include:

- New changes to be reviewed
- An update on implemented changes and failed changes
- Improvements to the change management process

5.6.4.4 Typical inputs

Integrated change advisory board inputs could include:

- Change requests and related information
- Change management process performance information

5.6.4.5 Typical outputs

Integrated change advisory board outputs could include:

- Change status updates
- Process improvements

5.7 Operational roles

An effective SIAM ecosystem is built on working relationships and cultural alignment between all the SIAM layers.

At an operational level, working groups, boards and process forums all help to establish relationships and encourage communication between service providers and the service integrator. These working groups, boards and process forums form structural elements of the SIAM ecosystem, spanning the SIAM layers; see **section 1** for more information.

There are many possible boards, process forums and working groups that can be implemented in a SIAM ecosystem, including:

- Integrated change advisory board

- Problem management forum
- Knowledge management forum
- Continual improvement forum
- Capacity management forum
- Information assurance and security forum
- Transition planning and support forum
- IT service continuity forum
- Service monitoring forum
- Incident management working group (for a specific incident or incidents)
- Release planning working group
- Problem management working group (for a specific problem or problems)
- Innovation working group (for a specific innovation)

The structural elements in place will vary in each SIAM ecosystem. A structural element can be created for any service management process or activity, if it supports improvements in service delivery and outcomes.

Forums can be combined where appropriate – for example, a single 'process improvement' forum could be used to assess possible improvements to multiple processes.

Combined forums are of value when processes have similar scope or have dependencies between their activities, for example change, configuration and release management. The number of meetings should always be balanced against the value of the meetings.

There are generic roles that will attend working groups and forums.

Process owner

- Accountable for end-to-end process design
- Accountable to process performance

Both the service integrator and the service providers will have process owners. The service integrator process owner will be accountable for end-to-end process integration across the service providers.

The service provider process owner will be accountable for a process within the service provider and for alignment with the end-to-end process. A process owner is a role, so one staff member may act as the process owner for multiple processes.

Process manager

- Responsible for process execution

In larger organizations, process manager roles are defined to support the process owner and be responsible for the execution of process activities.

Service owner

- Accountable for end-to-end service performance
- Defines service strategy

- Forecasts service demand and business requirements
- Service budget-holder

This role will typically be part of the customer organization.

Service manager

- Responsible for service delivery for one or more services

This role would typically be carried out by the service integrator.

Examples of operational roles

This section provides some examples of process forums and working groups in a SIAM ecosystem. These examples can be used as the basis for the design of other process forums and working groups within a SIAM model.

5.7.1 Knowledge management forum

The knowledge management forum is hosted and managed by the service integrator knowledge management process owner.

It is a regular forum where the performance and effectiveness of knowledge management across the ecosystem is reviewed and assessed.

5.7.1.1 Typical attendees

Knowledge management forum attendees could include:

- Service integrator knowledge management process owner (chair)
- Service provider knowledge management process owners/process managers
- Service integrator service manager as required
- Subject matter experts as required
- Customer representation as required

5.7.1.2 Typical frequency

Process forums are typically monthly.

5.7.1.3 Typical responsibilities

Knowledge management forum responsibilities could include:

- Reviewing accuracy and currency of the knowledge articles in use
- Identifying new knowledge articles that are required based on repeat incidents or requests received by the service desk
- Allowing service providers to collaborate on identifying any incident types that could be resolved at the service desk or via self-help systems rather than by second-line teams, improving the end-user experience

5.7.2 Continual improvement forum

The continual improvement forum is hosted and managed by the service integrator.

It is a cross-ecosystem forum attended by all service providers and the customer. Attendees can present, discuss and agree initiatives for improvement, for example ways to deliver cost savings or improve the customer experience.

5.7.2.1 Typical attendees

Continual improvement forum attendees could include:

- Service integrator continual improvement process owner (chair)
- Service provider continual improvement process owners/process managers
- Service integrator delivery manager/director
- Service owners
- Other process owners as required
- Subject matter experts as required
- Customer representation as required

5.7.2.2 Typical frequency

Process forums are typically monthly.

5.7.2.3 Typical responsibilities

Continual improvement forum responsibilities could include:

- Presenting and reviewing ideas for improvement
- Assessing the potential of initiatives
- Prioritization of initiatives
- Agreeing the responsible party or parties to implement the improvement; this may involve cross-service provider collaboration and implementation
- Approval of any budgetary spend (this may need to be escalated to a governance board)
- Communicating the benefits to the business
- Tracking the progress and ultimate success of the improvements

5.7.3 Major incident working group

The major incident working group is chaired and managed by the service integrator. It may also be referred to as a crisis team, critical incident team or major incident bridge.

It is convened during a major incident to coordinate the response, facilitate cross-service provider communication and provide regular updates to the customer organization.

Any lessons learned during a major incident will be discussed in the incident management process forum.

5.7.3.1 Typical attendees

Major incident working group attendees could include:

- Service integrator major incident manager (chair)
- Service provider incident management process owners/process managers
- Other process owners as required
- Subject matter and technical experts as required
- Service owners as required
- Customer representation as required

5.7.3.2 Typical frequency

A major incident working group will be held when required – when a major incident has occurred.

5.7.3.3 Typical responsibilities

Major incident working group responsibilities could include:

- Coordinating major incident investigation and resolution
- Coordinating major incident communications
- Encouraging a 'fix first, argue later' culture

5.8 The service desk in a SIAM ecosystem

The role of the service desk and how it is sourced will vary from SIAM ecosystem to ecosystem.

The service desk is often seen as a good candidate for external sourcing due to high staff turnover and management overhead, but some organizations prefer to keep it internal or use a hybrid approach.

The organization providing the service desk will be treated and managed as a service provider in the SIAM ecosystem, whether it is provided by the customer organization, the service integrator or a service provider.

Within a SIAM ecosystem, the service desk acts as a 'single source of truth' and provides important management information about service performance. If the service integrator is not providing the service desk, it must work very closely with it and use the service data it provides.

Some of the potential sourcing options are:

1. The customer organization provides the service desk and associated toolset, acting as an internal service provider, and routes incidents to service providers as necessary.
2. The service integrator provides the service desk and associated toolset.
3. An external service provider provides the service desk and toolset, but no other services.
4. An external service provider provides the service desk and toolset in addition to other services; this is often combined with end-user computing, applications or hosting.
5. Different service providers provide their own service desks and toolsets and the service integrator provides a consolidated view; this is only possible where it is clear to the customer which service desk to contact for support.

In most instances, the end user contacts a single service desk, which then works with the relevant service provider service desks and support teams. The end user has a single point of contact.

The staff who work on the service desk will require similar skills to those outside of a SIAM ecosystem, but they will also need:

- Supplier management skills
- Commercial awareness

These skills will allow them to work successfully with different service providers, which may have different contracts, service targets and responsibilities.

CHAPTER 6: SIAM PRACTICES

> Practices are defined as: *"the actual application or use of an idea, belief, or method, as opposed to theories relating to it."*[26]

From a SIAM perspective, 'practices' meet this definition when organizations are applying them within a SIAM model. The examples in this section give some illustrations of how to apply SIAM practices, principles and concepts to deliver value.

Within SIAM there are four types of practice:

1. People practices
2. Process practices
3. Measurement practices
4. Technology practices

This section of the BoK looks at one area for consideration in each practice type. It considers the challenges associated with that area, and then the working practices that can be used to address the challenges.

These example practices should not be thought of as 'good' or 'best' practice. They provide an illustration of how practices can work in a SIAM ecosystem.

For example, in **section 6.1** we consider cross-functional teams. Cross-functional teams are just one example of the challenges in a SIAM ecosystem and the people practices will help to deal with the challenges associated with cross-functional teams. Other challenges and practices exist and are explained in further detail in the SIAM Professional BoK[27].

SIAM also draws on practices from other areas of IT and management; see **section 4**.

6.1 People practices: Managing cross-functional teams

> *"A cross-functional team is a group of people with different functional expertise working toward a common goal. It may include people from finance, marketing, operations, and human resources departments. Typically, it includes employees from all levels of an organization."*[28]

---

[26] *www.lexico.com/definition/practice*.

[27] *www.itgovernancepublishing.co.uk/product/service-integration-and-management-siam-professional-body-of-knowledge-bok-second-edition*.

[28] Wikipedia, *https://en.wikipedia.org/wiki/Cross-functional_team*.

The SIAM ecosystem and cross-functional teams

With the SIAM ecosystem, cross-functional teams will have members from different organizations and different SIAM layers. These teams are referred to as "structural elements".

There are three types of structural element/cross-functional team:

1. Boards
2. Process forums
3. Working groups

These are described in **sections 1** and **5**.

In a SIAM environment, examples of cross-functional teams could include:

A major incident working group where the cause of an incident is unclear. The team includes staff from the service integrator and multiple service provider organizations. Team members need to work together towards a shared outcome (incident resolution), while meeting service requirements and balancing their own organizational goals.

The integrated change advisory board involving staff from the customer organization, service integrator and multiple service providers. The team members work together to review, prioritize, assess risk and approve or reject changes to an integrated service.

6.1.1 Challenges related to cross-functional teams

Some of the main challenges associated with cross-functional teams are:

1. Conflicting objectives, organizational strategies and working practices
2. Reluctance to share knowledge
3. Lack of automation

6.1.1.1 Conflicting objectives, organizational strategies and working practices

The cross-functional teams in a SIAM ecosystem contain staff from multiple service providers, the service integrator and, in some cases, the customer organization as well. This can create challenges when staff must balance their own organizational objectives with cross-functional team objectives.

For example, during a major incident, a service provider's organizational goals might be to demonstrate that it is not responsible for causing the incident, and to minimize the resources allocated to resolving it.

However, the end-to-end service targets could be focused on resolving the incident and then assessing what caused it later. This requires the service provider to adopt a 'fix first, argue later' approach, which may conflict with its individual organizational goals.

Differences between organizational strategies and working practices can also have an impact on the performance of a cross-functional team.

For example, technical organizations might prioritize resolving incidents above customer communication. In a SIAM ecosystem, they might have to prioritize customer communication over service restoration.

6.1.1.2 Reluctance to share

The service provider and service integrator staff working in a SIAM ecosystem need to share information, and collaborate at a people, process and technology level.

In an effective SIAM ecosystem, they may have targets relating to service improvement as well as service delivery.

To innovate effectively and improve service delivery, service providers and the service integrator need to work together. Some organizations may be reluctant to do this because they view it as sharing their intellectual property with a competitor.

6.1.1.3 Lack of automation

Lack of automation and ineffective toolsets can also be a challenge for cross-functional teams. Where more than one toolset is in use, poor integration between tools is also a challenge.

The issues here can include:

- Inability to measure end-to-end team performance
- Inability to easily share information between teams
- Duplicated work caused by entering data into multiple toolsets (the 'swivel chair' approach)
- Reduced likelihood of identifying patterns or opportunities for improvement
- Reduced workflow automation, leading to workflow interruptions, delays and an inability to monitor workflow

6.1.2 Practices for managing cross-functional teams

To support effective management of cross-functional teams, the service integrator and the customer need to consider:

1. Roles and responsibilities
2. Clear goals and objectives
3. Knowledge, data and information
4. Communication
5. Toolset integration

6.1.2.1 Roles and responsibilities

Defining clear principles and policies for roles and responsibilities as part of the Discovery & Strategy stage of the SIAM roadmap will lay the foundation for better cross-functional working.

This supports communication within cross-functional teams because all the parties involved have a clear understanding of who the stakeholders are.

RACI matrices are a useful tool for mapping roles and responsibilities in cross-functional teams.

RACI matrix

RACI matrices are used to manage resources and roles for the delivery of an activity or task. They can be used to identify all participants in the delivery of a process or function.

Resources can be drawn from different functional areas and organizations, so a RACI matrix is used to track who is doing what, identifying interfaces and engagement with other roles. It provides a clear mapping of roles across the different teams in the SIAM ecosystem.

RACI stands for Responsible, Accountable, Consulted and Informed.

Only one role can be **Accountable** for a task. The role that is accountable for the task has the overall authority – but might not carry out individual pieces of work themselves.

Any number of roles can be **Responsible** as part of the RACI model. These are the workers who will get the actual tasks done, and they will report to the Accountable resource about their progress.

Sometimes roles are **Consulted** to get a task done. This might be a person within the organization who holds specific knowledge, or it could be a document store or even an internet search engine. These resources need to be tracked to ensure they are available when required.

Other roles need to be **Informed**. These resources are stakeholders who need to track and understand exactly how the task is proceeding, or they may need an output from the activity. Customer organization sponsors, for example, will typically be informed about progress as part of a project.

To build a RACI matrix, these steps need to be followed:

- Identify activities
- Identify roles
- Assign RACI codes
- Identify gaps or overlaps that need resolving
- Distribute the chart for feedback
- Deploy to all relevant parties
- Monitor the roles
- Apply improvements or changes based on feedback and experience

6.1.2.2 Clear goals and objectives

As well as a clear understanding of roles and responsibilities, parties in a SIAM ecosystem need clear goals and objectives:

- The customer will define the strategic objectives for the services
- The objectives will be translated into contracts and service agreements
- The service integrator will work with service providers to:
  o Develop process goals and objectives that drive process execution
  o Develop operational-level agreements or targets that align with the contracts and service agreements

While it is important that each service provider has measurable service targets to work towards, they need to be part of an end-to-end performance management and reporting framework. This will, in turn, provide evidence of demonstrable achievement of service objectives, business benefits or value.

If there is no clear definition and communication of value, or end-to-end metrics, service providers may focus only on their own performance and not see the end-to-end view.

In some cases, it might be acceptable for a service provider to miss a target in one area, because it means meeting a target in a different area. The service integrator can help the service providers to prioritize when there is a conflict between individual targets and end-to-end service targets.

6.1.2.3 Knowledge, data and information

Cross-functional teams need access to shared knowledge, data and information.

When these are not shared or readily available:

- Team members will waste time rediscovering or recreating them
- Service issues and customer contacts might be managed in inconsistent ways
- Work will not be carried out in the most efficient way
- Different parties may have different 'versions of the truth'

The service integrator needs to create a knowledge management strategy and policy to govern how knowledge is gathered, processed, presented, managed and removed.

The service integrator will also make sure that all service providers have access to the knowledge they need as part of a shared knowledge repository. All service providers should contribute to this repository for the benefit of all other parties.

Checks need to be in place to make sure knowledge is updated, relevant and being used.

6.1.2.4 Communication

The service integrator and service providers need to communicate regularly and work to build relationships and trust. The RACI matrix developed as part of the roles and responsibilities definition is useful to define the 'who', 'what', 'when', 'where', 'how' and 'why' of communication.

A communication plan is key to ensure that:

- All stakeholders and their communication requirements are identified
- There is an appropriate level of regular communication for all stakeholders, for example meetings and levels of reporting
- Communication takes place at the right level for each layer of the SIAM ecosystem
- Communication is consistent across service providers
- Effective communication channels are selected to support timeliness, relationship building, ease of execution and access

Use of the various structural elements in the SIAM ecosystem (including boards, process forums and working groups) will help to build relationships and encourage better cross-functional working.

Virtual teams

In a SIAM ecosystem, team members are likely to be in different geographical locations. These are referred to as 'virtual teams'.

The resources in the teams might also have multiple customers to work with; for example, a service provider's technical support staff might be involved in more than one SIAM engagement.

The service integrator needs to carefully consider how to manage communication within these teams. Even more care is required if teams are virtual as well as cross-functional.

Virtual teams need to build relationships between team members. This can be challenging if there is no regular face-to-face contact between them. It is recommended to have at least one face-to-face event where team members can get to know each other, to foster trust and to create good working relationships.

Tools can be used to support communication in virtual teams. Examples are videoconferencing, social media and chat tools.

6.1.2.5 Toolset integration

For cross-functional teams, integration between toolsets will save time and resources, and reduce the possibility of errors. It can also support workflow automation.

Integrating toolsets will reduce the need to re-enter and translate data. There is less chance of information errors leading to friction between teams.

6.2 Process practices: Integrating processes across service providers

Within the context of this document, a process is "a documented, repeatable approach to carrying out a series of tasks or activities".

SIAM environments and integrated processes

In a SIAM environment, processes must operate effectively and efficiently across multiple parties. This includes service providers, the service integrator and, sometimes, the customer.

For example, during change management, the service integrator is accountable for changes to integrated services, across all the service providers involved with the change.

Change management includes change recording, assessment, prioritization, planning, approval and post-implementation reviews.

The service providers, service integrator and, potentially, customer will all be involved. This requires a change management process that is integrated across all parties.

6.2.1 Challenges related to integrating processes across service providers

Challenges associated with integrating processes across service providers include:

1. Service providers do not integrate their processes or share process details

2. Gaps between process activities
3. Time-consuming and manual reporting
4. Poor relationships between service providers/a blame culture

6.2.1.1 Service providers do not integrate their processes or share process details

Within a SIAM ecosystem, data and information must flow between all parties. This does not mean that all parties must use the same process. Instead, each service provider and the service integrator must work together to ensure their processes are aligned to deliver the required outcome.

This requires processes from the service providers, service integrator and customer to be aligned and integrated. Some of the service providers in a SIAM ecosystem may be unwilling, or unable, to make the adaptations necessary to support this integration.

This may be acceptable if outcomes and performance meet the predefined targets. However, unless this is considered in the design of the integrated processes, it can result in:

- Adversely affected outcomes
- Failure to meet end-to-end service level
- Inefficiencies in the execution of the integrated processes
- Unforeseen additional overheads in the service integrator
- Miscommunication

For example, consider a situation where one of the services is a cloud-based commodity email service.

The service provider will publish planned changes and service outages on its website. It will not directly inform the service integrator, seek approval for changes or attend any change management boards. The service integrator must regularly check the service provider's website. The service integrator informs the other service providers and customer of any changes that will affect them.

6.2.1.2 Gaps between process activities

Process integration fails when there is a gap or break in the process flow.

This could be a simple action; for example, an incident being assigned to a queue for a service provider, and not being picked up, resulting in increased downtime for the customer. Gaps are often identified when process performance targets are failed, for example when incident resolution times are missed.

These gaps need to be identified and addressed during Plan & Build and on an ongoing basis. The development and agreement of process flows and RACI matrices (see **section 6.1.2**) will help to identify and avoid such gaps.

Gaps should also be identified during the service integrator assurance activities.

6.2.1.3 Time-consuming and manual reporting

Where different providers use different processes, it is likely that they will also use different toolsets. The use of different toolsets can affect the ability, effectiveness and efficiency of the monitoring of and reporting on performance of end-to-end processes.

Unless this is recognized and managed during the Plan & Build stage, monitoring and reporting for end-to-end processes can be time consuming and laborious. Design activities must recognize this, to ensure that the value of the information produced justifies the effort required to collect and process it.

6.2.1.4 Poor relationships between service providers/a blame culture

The success of an integrated process depends on all parties contributing to its design, execution and improvement. Service providers are less likely to contribute if their relationships with other service providers and with the service integrator are poor.

Service providers need to adopt a 'fix first, argue later' mentality to resolve issues. This needs to be supported by a 'no blame' culture so that service providers are ready to be open about their faults, rather than trying to hide them.

The 'no blame' culture needs to start with the customer and then be continually reinforced by the service integrator to create a collaborative environment. This will assist with building the necessary good relationships.

6.2.2 Practices for integrating processes across service providers

Practices for integrating processes across service providers include:

1. Focusing on process outcomes
2. Continual process improvement
3. Establishing process forums

In addition to these practices, the RACI matrices mentioned in **section 6.1.2** will also be helpful for identifying the role and responsibility of each stakeholder for each process activity.

6.2.2.1 Focus on process outcomes

The service integrator needs to be clear about the outcome that a process is expected to deliver. This can then be communicated to the service providers so that they all understand their role and responsibilities within the process.

It is better to start with the outcome and then work back, rather than to start with lower-level steps and activities in the hope that they can be brought together into a process. For each process that involves multiple parties, these items should be documented and understood:

- Inputs
- Outputs
- Outcomes
- Interactions
- Dependencies
- Controls
- Data and information standards
- Process steps
- Process flow

RACI matrices can help to document these, and are a commonly used and widely understood technique.

It is important to recognize and reward positive outcomes when processes are performing well.

6.2.2.2 Continual process improvement

All processes should be subject to review and improvement measures. This continual improvement can be managed on multiple levels:

- Within each area responsible for the provision and fulfilment of the process
- At the process level, for example via the process forums or the process owner

These levels should also feed into an overall process improvement program run by the service integrator. This is particularly relevant when an improvement is dependent on resources external to the process or is likely to have a significantly beneficial impact.

Each process will have a process owner who will be accountable for continual improvement across the end-to-end process, and the service integrator has ultimate accountability for process improvement.

Process improvements should be assessed, justified and approved using an agreed mechanism, often in the process forum. Once improvements are implemented, their benefits should be tracked to confirm a change has been delivered. This can be more challenging in a SIAM ecosystem than for a process that exists within a single organization.

6.2.2.3 Establishing process forums

Process forums are a type of structural element within a SIAM model. They are used to bring together process owners and practitioners from the service providers and the service integrator. Their purpose is to work together on the design and improvement of how their (process-)activities support end-to-end delivery.

This includes:

- Defining data and information standards
- Identifying and managing process improvements
- Developing and sharing good practice
- Sharing information
- Assessing and improving capability and maturity

Process forums are invaluable for building relationships and trust between all parties. They can be established for a single process, a group of related processes, or a practice in the SIAM ecosystem.

6.3 Measurement practices: Enable and report on end-to-end services

End-to-end service measurement refers to the ability to monitor an actual service, not just its individual technical components or providers. Effective measurement practices support the performance management and reporting framework.

SIAM environments and end-to-end service measurement

In a SIAM environment, examples of end-to-end measurement could include:

- **The percentage of service downtime related to failed changes:** based on the amount of downtime (minutes, hours, days) and the percentage of this caused by changes
- **Responsiveness of the service against defined targets:** based on measuring the customer's actual experience of the service, not just individual elements, such as network speed or application responsiveness

End-to-end measurement is more complex in a SIAM environment because more than one service provider is involved with service delivery. The end-to-end view is aggregated by the service integrator using data from all service providers.

6.3.1 Challenges related to enabling and reporting on end-to-end services

Challenges associated with measurement of end-to-end services include:

1. Lack of strategic requirements
2. Reluctance to share information
3. Inability to map service architecture or end-to-end workflow
4. Not measuring the correct amount of data and information

6.3.1.1 Lack of strategic requirements

An effective performance management and reporting framework can only be built once it is clear what needs to be measured.

If the overall strategic requirements for the services are unknown, it will be difficult to create a meaningful set of end-to-end measurements and reports.

6.3.1.2 Reluctance to share information

Poor relationships or competitive tension between service providers can lead to an unwillingness to share information. Service providers might also be reluctant to share information if they feel it will be used to punish them, rather than as a source of learning and improvement.

In some situations, the customer withholds information from the service integrator. If the service integrator is an external organization, for example, the customer might not want to share some information that it considers confidential.

6.3.1.3 Inability to map end-to-end service architecture

Many organizations struggle to map an end-to-end service, and understand what is in scope for measurement and what is not. With the addition of multiple service providers and a distributed architecture, this can be even more challenging.

The service integrator needs to map the end-to-end service and work with each service provider to confirm what needs to be measured to build the end-to-end picture. Enabling practices like OBASHI and configuration management can help.

6.3.1.4 Not measuring the correct amount of data and information

Some organizations do not collect enough data, and some collect too much.

If an organization does not collect enough, there is a risk that important information will be missed. If it collects too much, there is a risk that there is too much data to analyze, which can also lead to important information being missed.

The same is true for how much information is included in reports. Small amounts of information may seem easier to understand but may hide important information. Large amounts may be difficult to understand and can complicate the ability to present an accurate picture.

The challenge is to identify the optimum amount of information to collect and report on. A useful technique is to report at a summary level but have the detailed reports available to support any requirement for more in-depth information.

6.3.2 Practices for enabling and reporting on end-to-end services

Practices for enabling and reporting on end-to-end services include:

1. Create a performance management and reporting framework
2. Make reports visual
3. Use quantitative and qualitative measures; and
4. Apply agile thinking

6.3.2.1 Create a performance management and reporting framework

A performance management and reporting framework provides a way to structure data and information from service measurement and link them to the customer organization's strategic requirements.

The performance management and reporting framework will be created during the Plan & Build roadmap stage.

Performance management and reporting frameworks can be structured in a variety of ways, depending on the available toolset, strategic requirements and service contracts.

Possible framework structures include:

- By SIAM ecosystem layers:
  - Service provider metrics
  - Service integrator metrics
  - Customer metrics
- By type:
  - People metrics
  - Process metrics
  - Technology metrics
- By hierarchy, allowing for information to be expanded or shown in more detail when needed:
  - Strategic metrics
  - Tactical metrics
  - Operational metrics

6.3.2.2 Make reports visual

Information is most effective when it is visual and easy to understand. Using service dashboards and scorecards will increase the impact of reporting.

A picture can be easier to understand than a long report, but care must be taken to clearly identify each visual and what it indicates.

6.3.2.3 Use quantitative and qualitative measures

Quantitative measures are numerical, and factual; for example, the number of incidents that were resolved in the agreed timescales, or a reduction in the number of target breaches.

Qualitative measures are usually descriptive and often in non-numerical form; for example, customer satisfaction surveys.

While it is relatively easy to measure and report on quantitative measures, they do not often reflect the quality of the service accurately. One of the drivers for SIAM is the 'watermelon' effect, where service providers report they are meeting all their targets, but the customer is still not happy. Using a mix of quantitative and qualitative measures will help to provide a balanced view. Care should be taken to ensure that these remain aligned to strategic requirements and service objectives.

The watermelon effect

The watermelon effect occurs when a report is 'green on the outside, red on the inside'.

The service provider(s) meet individual targets, but the end-to-end service is not meeting the customer's requirements. This does not deliver a good outcome for the customer, and should also be a concern for the service provider.

It may be good for the service provider to be meeting its targets, but if the customer is not happy, it will not have a good long-term relationship.

In this situation, the target is not aligned to business requirements.

6.3.2.4 Apply agile thinking

The application of Agile techniques can help to determine the optimum amount of information in reports. Start by reporting on a minimum set of viable metrics. These can provide the minimum amount of information to assess performance, with no unnecessary additions or duplication.

These reports can then be used as the basis for discussion and learning, with more measurements being added if required.

It is often beneficial to start small and then develop the performance management and reporting framework. This approach should initially use less resource than trying to measure every single element of the ecosystem.

See **section 4.5** for more information about SIAM and Agile.

6.4 Technology practices: creating a tooling strategy

A tooling strategy outlines the requirements for a toolset or toolsets to support the SIAM ecosystem. It will include functional and non-functional requirements, the processes that need to be supported, standards for interfacing with the toolset(s) and a roadmap for future development.

Typically, organizations will focus on the IT service management tool, which will support processes including incident, problem, change, configuration, release management and request fulfilment. However, there are other areas where a tooling strategy will provide considerable benefit, such as:

- Event management
- Event correlation
- Software asset management
- Discovery
- Capacity, performance and availability management
- Operational risk management
- Project management
- Service performance reporting

SIAM environments and the tooling strategy

An optimized tooling strategy will make it easier for the service providers in a SIAM ecosystem to work together. It can also:

- Help the service integrator get a 'real time' view of end-to-end service performance
- Improve the efficiency of workflow
- Support data integration, which is critical in establishing aggregated service views from data provided by multiple service providers

There are several possible approaches for tooling. These are listed in **section 2**. The aim is to have integration between all toolsets.

Integration is difficult to achieve, relying on sophisticated data mapping between service providers and the service integrator. Toolset integration requirements need to be documented and assessed in the context of the broader technology architecture.

In some circumstances, it may be acceptable to use less sophisticated and more manual methods (often referred to as 'loose coupling' of data exchange). For time-critical activities like major incident management, there may be little alternative other than to build integration between toolsets (referred to as 'tight coupling' of data exchange).

The integrated toolset acts as a single version of the truth for all the parties in the SIAM ecosystem, simplifying data transfer, reporting and accuracy.

6.4.1 Challenges related to creating a tooling strategy

Challenges associated with creating a tooling strategy include:

1. Ineffective legacy tools

2. Defining the toolset scope
3. Non-compliant service providers
4. Lack of architecture

6.4.1.1 Ineffective legacy tools

The customer organization may require the service integrator and/or service providers to use legacy toolsets that it already has in place. This can lead to several challenges:

- The toolset may not support all the processes in the SIAM ecosystem
- It may not support the use of integrated processes
- It will contain legacy data, which may be challenging to adapt to the new environment
- It may be difficult to interface with the service provider's and service integrator's toolset
- If the service integrator is external, it may not have any expertise in the toolset

6.4.1.2 Defining the toolset scope

A SIAM ecosystem can include many processes, some of which are outside the 'standard' set of IT service management processes.

The tooling strategy should encompass all the processes in the SIAM model, and recognize that the ideal solution may be a hybrid of various tools, to support the functional requirements of each process and the broader SIAM ecosystem.

The toolset also needs to support end-to-end process control, not just operational execution. More tool vendors are now creating functionality that supports a SIAM ecosystem.

6.4.1.3 Non-compliant service providers

If the tooling strategy requires that all parties use the same toolsets, some potential service providers may be unwilling to be part of the SIAM ecosystem.

If the tooling strategy is that service providers integrate their own tools with the service integrator's toolset, some may be unwilling or unable to configure the integration. For example, providers of commodity cloud services may have little flexibility in their offerings.

The tooling strategy needs careful consideration at the Discovery & Strategy and Plan & Build stages of the SIAM Roadmap, as it has influence on and dependencies within the SIAM structures and the overall SIAM model. The strategy must also consider the data and information standards.

Once they have been agreed, requirements from the tooling strategy should be included in any contracts with service providers and any external service integrator. This is because a non-compliant service provider can lead to inefficiencies in cross-provider processes and reporting, and gaps between service providers.

6.4.1.4 Lack of architecture

The absence of an enterprise architecture and technical architecture for the SIAM ecosystem and services will create challenges related to the selection of toolsets, and the definition of interfaces between toolsets.

The architecture documents need to address:

- The need for data sovereignty/visibility requirements to be addressed through role-based access controls. For example, service providers may not be able to view each other's targets or performance.
- The need for robust data integration capabilities. Some organizations choose to build an 'enterprise service bus' or messaging engine into their technology architectures to cater for this requirement
- The need for all data update activities to be auditable and traceable.
- The need for all parties in the SIAM ecosystem to be familiar with the tooling strategy and the specific tools to be deployed, not only so they can develop any integrations as necessary but also to ensure that their staff are trained adequately in their use.

The toolset architecture must support the tooling strategy.

The service providers of the toolsets themselves must be treated as a service provider within the SIAM ecosystem, because the effective operation of the SIAM model is dependent on their services.

6.4.2 Practices related to creating a tooling strategy

Practices associated with creating a tooling strategy include:

1. Technology strategy and roadmap
2. Industry-standard integration methods
3. Ownership of data and toolsets
4. Ease of adding and removing service providers
5. Adopting a common data dictionary

6.4.2.1 Technology strategy and roadmap

The customer organization needs to outline its technology strategy and roadmap to help the service integrator and service providers understand how the SIAM toolset will integrate and evolve.

The customer also needs to share any functional and technical requirements, for example if the toolset must meet certain security specifications.

6.4.2.2 Industry-standard integration methods

Using industry-standard integration methods will make it easier for service providers to share information between their own tools and an integrated SIAM toolset. This will simplify interface creation and should reduce the need for expensive development and customization.

The integration approach adopted should not just cater for data transmission, but also for error handling in the event of issues occurring.

Given the potential criticality of the integration, consideration should also be given to service continuity requirements. Both the production and any backup or continuity environments should be tested to ensure that they meet the functional and non-functional requirements required by the customer.

6.4.2.3 Ownership of data and toolsets

When the service integrator role is being taken by an external organization, the tooling strategy needs to clarify who owns the toolset, and the data within it.

If the external service integrator owns the toolset (for example), the customer needs to ensure it still has data access if the commercial relationship ends, or define how the data will be migrated at such time.

In addition, the toolset must be placed under change control, particularly if data integration exists. If changes to toolsets are made by any party, this can have unexpected effects on the integrity of the supporting data integrations described above, if data fields or values change.

6.4.2.4 Ease of adding and removing service providers

One of the benefits of a SIAM ecosystem is the ability to add and remove service providers easily.

The tooling strategy needs to support this. When a new service provider is added, it needs to be easy for that organization to adopt the toolset, including set-up of local toolset interfaces and training its staff.

When a service provider is removed, it must be simple to remove its access to the toolset and ensure that data is stored or (re)moved as required.

6.4.2.5 Adopting a common data dictionary

The toolset should be used to enforce a common data dictionary. This will deliver several benefits, for example giving consistency and a common understanding of incident priority and severity classifications.

There will be confusion if one service provider's 'priority 1' incident is another service provider's 'severity 3'. This activity should be undertaken for all data fields in the toolset.

The data dictionary must be in place before the SIAM model is operational, as it supports the exchange of data and information across the SIAM ecosystem.

The need for a common data dictionary must be part of the tooling strategy, as the selected toolsets must be able to support its use.

CHAPTER 7: SIAM CULTURAL CONSIDERATIONS

The SIAM ecosystem and the relationships between the customer organization, service integrator and service providers create a unique environment. From sourcing and contractual negotiations through to governance and operational management, there are specific SIAM considerations.

The cultural aspects of a transition to SIAM are one such consideration. An effective SIAM ecosystem is underpinned by effective relationships and appropriate behaviors. The ecosystem culture needs to encourage and reinforce these relationships and behaviors.

SIAM is often described as a sourcing strategy, but it is more than this. It extends beyond sourcing into the ongoing management and improvement of the service to deliver better business outcomes.

Service providers that compete in other areas of a market may find themselves working together to meet overall customer objectives in a SIAM ecosystem. Some service providers might be internal departments of the customer organization, working together with external service providers.

There are specific challenges when an external organization is fulfilling the service integrator role, because it is governing service providers that may also be its competitors.

The cultural considerations examined in this section are:

1. Cultural change
2. Collaboration and cooperation
3. Cross-service provider organization

7.1 Cultural change

7.1.1 What does this mean in a SIAM environment?

An organization that moves from either an insourced or a traditional outsourced environment to an environment based on SIAM will undergo a large program of change and transformation. If the cultural aspects of the change are not managed effectively, it can create disruption in the customer organization.

Adopting a new SIAM structure can include internal role changes in the customer organization and staff being transferred from the customer organization to the service providers or the service integrator. This can have a significant impact on staff at a personal level; they will be concerned about their role, their career and their skillsets.

Moving to an environment that includes multiple service providers will require the customer organization to build SIAM expertise and capabilities, understanding of the ecosystem and technical landscape, and the future technical roadmap and strategy. This expertise and knowledge might already exist in the organization, but in many transitions to SIAM it does not. Staff will need commercial, contractual and supplier management skills, in addition to more traditional service management skills.

Cultural change will also come from a change of management style. The customer organization needs to manage service provider performance at an executive, not an operational level. Its role is to step in and resolve contractual issues when required and to provide corporate governance. This is a shift away from managing activities to managing outcomes; in other words, managing the 'what', not the 'how'.

The customer organization needs to empower its service integrator to manage the service providers at the operational level. These changes in relationship dynamics and responsibilities will lead to, and depend on, changes in culture.

For the service providers, culture change is driven by the need to work collaboratively. All the service providers need to work with the service integrator and with other service providers towards the shared goal.

7.1.2 Why is it important?

No organizational change can succeed without cultural change. If the culture and organizational behaviors stay the same, new processes and ways of working will not be adopted and expected benefits will not be delivered.

Effective management of cultural change will provide the basis for a successful SIAM transformation program, and will help the customer to retain skilled and motivated staff in key roles.

7.1.3 What challenges will be faced?

Some of the challenges related to cultural change are:

- Staff who are moving to a new organization can experience concern at a professional and at a personal, emotional level. Professionally, there will be a level of uncertainty over their role and their skills and, emotionally, they will be concerned about the possible impact on their life and career. This can lead to staff leaving, absenteeism and loyalty issues.
- Organizations can suffer from change fatigue if too much is happening at once, leading to a higher chance of changes failing and new behaviors not being adopted.
- People continue using old processes or move back to old ways of working. It is important for every stakeholder in the SIAM ecosystem to reinforce behaviors; for example, at the service provider level, staff need to be encouraged to contact the service integrator, and not the customer.
- The customer organization's own business outcomes may be affected negatively if the changes are disruptive and have an impact on service delivery.

7.1.4 How can they be resolved?

These cultural issues can be addressed in several ways, including:

- Having a clear definition of the SIAM model and all associated roles and responsibilities at organization, team and individual levels.
- From the customer perspective:
  o Implementing a good business change or organizational change management process, reinforced with a strong communication plan to prevent misinformation and rumors spreading.
  o Applying program management to the SIAM roadmap, tracking progress and identifying where course corrections are needed to help increase confidence in likely success.
  o Considering the use of external consultancy to provide guidance, advice and an objective view.
  o Understanding what retained capabilities are needed and putting plans in place to keep the skilled people in their roles.

- From the customer and service integrator perspective, implementing a strong overarching governance structure, supported by processes, which work in practice and not just in theory.
- From the service integrator and service provider perspective, aligning their own communication plans with the overall communication plan and measuring the effectiveness of communication.
- From a service provider perspective, understanding the organizations it will be working with and how they want to work together, and committing to the level of collaboration required in a SIAM environment.

7.1.5 Cultural change and the SIAM structures

Externally sourced	The key challenge for this structure relates to staff who are moving from the customer organization to another organization as part of the transition to SIAM; the professional and personal impact will need to be managed.
Internally sourced	To deliver effective cultural change and a successful transition to SIAM, the customer organization will need skilled people. These may not exist within the organization and could be difficult to recruit.
Lead supplier	As with the externally sourced service integrator structure, the key challenge for this structure relates to staff who are moving from the customer organization to another organization as part of the transition to SIAM; the professional and personal impact will need to be managed.
Hybrid	The key challenge for this structure is that confusion about roles and responsibilities can make it difficult for staff from the customer organization to change their behavior; this applies if the interfaces between the customer and external organization at the service integrator level are not clearly defined. Staff need to be clear on their role and the role of the service integrator's employees.

7.2 Collaboration and cooperation

7.2.1 What does this mean in a SIAM ecosystem?

In many cases, a transition to SIAM means that service providers that are used to competing must work together to deliver customer outcomes. This often requires a change in mindset. The service providers must work together; the relationship moves from competitive to collaborative.

In an outsourced environment with no service integration element, service providers may pursue their own objectives. Silos and a blame culture are commonplace. Within a SIAM ecosystem, the focus is on relationships, particularly cross-provider relationships, governance controls and pursuit of common goals, rather than achievement of specific individual organizational service levels and objectives.

In a SIAM ecosystem, service providers need to put competitive considerations aside and adapt to a new way of working. The customer and the service integrator also need to be clear on their role and the boundaries of their responsibilities. These organizations are also likely to be working in new ways.

Cultural considerations for collaboration and cooperation include:

- Fix first, argue later: when there is an issue affecting service, the service providers need to work together rather than assign blame or pass issues around.
- Service providers must acknowledge that the service integrator is the voice of the customer, and has the autonomy to direct and make decisions and govern without being undermined.
- From the customer's perspective, it needs to empower the service integrator to manage the service providers, and not interfere or duplicate effort.
- Creating an environment that is focused on business outcomes and the customer, not on an individual service provider's contracts and agreements.

7.2.2 Why is it important?

In a SIAM ecosystem, the service integrator does not usually have a contractual relationship with the service providers, but it does need to be able to manage and govern their behavior on behalf of the customer.

If the parties in the ecosystem are not prepared to collaborate, the service integrator will not be able to control service delivery effectively.

For example, it will be very challenging for the service integrator to manage a major incident from end to end and within service targets if the service providers will not provide information or accept responsibility for investigation.

7.2.3 What challenges will be faced?

Some of the challenges related to collaboration and cooperation include:

- From the service integrator's perspective, the challenge of service providers bypassing it and going straight to the customer. The customer needs to support the service integrator by reinforcing correct communication paths, and the service integrator needs to build relationships and reiterate correct ways of working.
- From the service provider's perspective:
  - o 'Fix first, argue later' being abused so that it incurs additional costs. This can happen if issues are identified and not corrected by the customer or the service integrator, so that the service provider must deal with them repeatedly.
  - o Being reluctant to collaborate and share with the other service providers.
- Trust is a critical success factor for collaboration and cooperation. Trust between service providers (some of which may be internal, and some external), trust between the service providers and the service integrator, and trust between the service integrator and the customer must be built and maintained.
- In a SIAM ecosystem that includes internal and external service providers, the internal service providers are part of the same organization as the customer. They may be reluctant to collaborate with the service integrator and with the external service providers; they may also have less mature delivery capabilities and so are less able to cooperate.
- In a SIAM ecosystem that includes internal and external service providers, the internal service providers will not have the same contractual imperatives that require them to collaborate.

7.2.4 How can they be resolved?

These cultural issues can be addressed in several ways, including:

- For all parties:
  - Creating a 'code of conduct' or 'rules of the club' agreement, with input from all parties in the SIAM ecosystem. These govern behaviors on a day-to-day basis; for example: how staff will behave in meetings, they will maintain professional and courteous behavior always, and they will attend forums and make effective contributions. (See **section 7.2.4.1**.)
  - Signing collaboration agreements that are part of each contract, or agreed between parties after the contract is signed, to add more detail about how they will work together. (See **section 7.2.4.2**.)
- Between the service integrator and each of the service providers, use operational-level agreements (OLAs) to break down service targets and agreements into more detail, helping them to understand their role and their interfaces with other parts of the ecosystem and when collaboration and cooperation is required. (See **section 7.2.4.3**.)

7.2.4.1 Example code of conduct

A code of conduct (or 'rules of the club') document is not a contractual agreement. It provides high-level guidance describing how the parties in the SIAM ecosystem will work together. All the parties can then hold each other to account, for example highlighting if someone is behaving unacceptably in a meeting.

This will not usually be a formal document, and is normally brief, often only a single page. Where required, it may also include:

- Title page
- Document control: author, date, status, version, change log, etc.
- Contents
- Introduction and document purpose
- Parties to the document
- Validity
- Approval/signatories

The suggested key content is:

Partnership aims

- What are the expected business outcomes?
- What is the SIAM ecosystem meant to deliver?

For example:

- Better value for money
- Greater efficiency and cost-effectiveness
- Greater flexibility to respond to evolving business requirements

Partnership ethos

- What values do the parties need to uphold?

For example:

- Maintain professionalism
- Work together as one team
- Share knowledge and ideas
- Embrace change
- Put the customer first
- Be courteous/respectful to others

7.2.4.2 Example collaboration agreement

An effective collaboration agreement will help to create a culture based on working together to deliver shared outcomes, without continual reference back to contracts.

Collaboration agreements should be used with care. They should set out the intent of how service providers are expected to collaborate with each other, and with the service integrator.

Sufficient detail should be included to avoid ambiguity, and to reduce the likelihood of future disputes when a service provider was not aware of a specific collaboration requirement, for example the need to take an active role in process forums.

Consideration must be given to the remedial approach that will be used if one of the parties does not align with the collaboration agreement. This can form part of the contract with the customer, but, to be truly effective, the parties should embrace the collaboration agreement as part of the SIAM culture, and not see it as a contractual requirement.

A typical collaboration agreement will contain the following sections:

- Title page
- Document control: author, date, status, version, change log, etc.
- Contents
- Introduction
- Document purpose
- Parties to the document
- Validity period
- Termination
- Required behaviors: for example, avoid unnecessary duplication of effort, do not hinder or withhold information from other service providers
- Mechanisms to support collaboration: for example, commitment to support process forums to review, improve and innovate processes and service delivery; commitment to triage and work together to resolve issues/challenges when requested by the service integrator; commitment to be involved in reviews and assurance activities
- Where relevant, toolsets to support collaboration

- Expected areas of collaboration: for example, review of proposed changes, incident investigation, taking part in working groups, innovation
- Dependencies between parties
- Any non-financial/non-contractual remedies: for example, where one or more service providers agrees with the service integrator and the customer to carry out actions to address an issue rather than trigger a contractual target and accept a financial penalty
- Change control
- Dispute resolution and escalation points

7.2.4.3 Example operational-level agreement

Operational-level agreements (OLAs) between the service integrator and service providers break down service targets into more detail. They include guidelines and common ways of working that support effective integration and delivery across the ecosystem. While the contents of OLAs are not themselves contractual obligations (all contracts are held by the customer organization), they should be formal agreements that are documented and controlled.

OLAs support end-to-end service delivery. For example, end-to-end incident management might include a four-hour resolution time for priority 1 incidents. In the OLA, the service provider might agree to a target of 30 minutes to either accept an incident or pass the information to a different service provider.

Within a SIAM ecosystem, it is important to define each service and its associated targets fully. OLAs support that definition and provide control and visibility. OLAs are prepared by the service integrator with input from the service providers. The service provider referenced in the OLA must have agreed the contents. The OLA supports the customer organization's overall objectives, but the customer organization may not be interested in the document detail.

OLAs can also be set up between two or more service providers, to agree or add some detail about how they work together.

An OLA should include content such as:

- Title page
- Document control: author, date, status, version, change log, etc.
- Contents
- Introduction
- Document purpose
- Parties to the document
- Validity
- Approval/signatories
- Rules for OLA termination
- Rules for OLA governance and escalation criteria
- Review schedule
- OLA change management
- Service description
- Scope of OLA: in- and out-of-scope activities

- Dependent services
- OLA details:
  - Name of service (for example, service desk, capacity management)
  - Service description
  - Service hours
  - Service provider
  - Service consumers
  - Service outcomes
  - Contact points and roles
  - Agreed activities of all parties (for example, party A will send an incident record to party B, party B will confirm receipt)
  - Service targets
  - Measurement: availability, performance targets, etc.
  - RACI matrix
- Service boundaries
- Quality assurance and service reporting
- Service reviews
- Glossary

7.2.5 Collaboration and cooperation and the SIAM structures

Externally sourced	• Internal service providers may be unwilling to collaborate and cooperate with the external service integrator.
Internally sourced	• External service providers may be more willing to collaborate and cooperate as they will perceive the service integrator as the customer. • There is a risk that a customer organization might not manage the service providers well owing to a lack of SIAM experience. If the service integrator cannot encourage the right culture and behaviors, this will affect the level of collaboration and cooperation. • If the internal service integrator is seen to treat internal service providers differently, this can lead to reduced collaboration and cooperation by the external service providers. • Internal service providers may be unwilling to collaborate and cooperate with the internal service integrator.
Lead supplier	• Internal service providers may be unwilling to collaborate and cooperate with the external service integrator. • If the lead supplier is seen to favor its own service provider in its service integrator role, this can lead to reduced collaboration and cooperation from the other service providers.
Hybrid	• The roles and responsibilities of the customer acting as service integrator and the third-party service integrator need to be clear. It is challenging for service providers to collaborate if they do not understand the structure and boundaries of responsibilities.

	• Internal service providers may be unwilling to collaborate and cooperate with the hybrid service integrator because it includes external elements.

7.3 Cross-service provider organization

This section addresses the cultural aspects of cross-service provider organization only. For more detail about managing cross-functional teams and managing conflict, see **section 6.1**.

Cross-service provider organization describes the cultural considerations associated with managing a service across multiple service providers.

7.3.1 What does this mean in a SIAM ecosystem?

The SIAM ecosystem can include an internal, hybrid, external, or lead supplier service integrator, plus several internal or external service providers.

Each service provider will have its own strategies, objectives and ways of working. The customer organization does not always have the ability (or desire) to mandate that all service providers follow a common set of processes or use the same toolset. They do, however, require all service providers to be able to interface with and integrate into the end-to-end service management processes.

From a cultural perspective, cross-service provider organization requires service providers to have appropriate behaviors and attitudes to support the customer organization and help it achieve its goals, rather than focusing on individual goals.

7.3.2 Why is it important?

Successful cross-service provider organization supports delivery of the end-to-end service. It starts with the customer organization. The customer needs to articulate a clear vision of what success looks like to all the service providers in the SIAM ecosystem.

The vision needs to be cascaded through all layers and across the ecosystem. This will then enable consistent:

- Strategies
- Objectives
- Processes: this does not preclude service providers using their own processes and procedures, but assures that the overall end-to-end process is integrated, can be managed, and is driving the correct outcomes

7.3.3 What challenges will be faced?

Some of the cultural challenges related to cross-service provider organization include:

- The customer retained organization may step back into its old role and get involved with delivery, rather than focusing on corporate governance and its own business objectives. This creates confusion and duplication, and does not allow the service providers, service integrator or customer to work effectively.
- Service providers focus on their own targets at the expense of end-to-end service targets.

- Service providers do not subscribe to the culture of collaboration and do not share innovations and potential improvements with other parts of the ecosystem.
- The service integrator does not treat service providers equally, leading to resentment and disengagement.
- If service providers have poor interfaces with end-to-end service management processes and tools, the role of the service integrator becomes more challenging; for example, monitoring, reporting, measurement will all be less effective.

7.3.4 How can they be resolved?

These cultural issues can be addressed in several ways, including:

- For all parties:
  - o Establishing consistent contractual targets/service level agreements and common performance measures/key performance indicators across the supply chain, so that all service providers feel they are equal and not disadvantaged.
  - o Having performance measures that encourage partnering and shared innovation with other parties.
  - o Cross-service provider processes must be based on a common language that all parties can understand.
- From the customer perspective, empowering the service integrator to have ownership, responsibility and accountability.
- From the customer, service integrator and service provider perspective, celebrate success, and praise excellent service performance, delivery and innovation to emphasize and reward the desired behaviors.
- Establish 'champion' process forums with representation from the service integrator and all service providers to discuss and improve the effectiveness of end-to-end processes, tools, interfaces and integration.

7.3.5 Cross-service provider organization and the SIAM structures

Externally sourced	External service providers may be reluctant to share information about how they work with an external service integrator, if they view them as a competitor.
Internally sourced	Internal service providers may be unwilling to work with and integrate with external service providers.
Lead supplier	The external organization that is acting as the service integrator and a service provider could be seen as a 'favorite' of the customer. If other service providers do not feel they are being treated fairly, they are less likely to work together.
Hybrid	Effective cross-service provider organization requires clear direction from the customer and service integrator. If the roles within the hybrid service

	integrator are not clearly defined, meetings and structures to support cross-service provider organization may not be put in place.

CHAPTER 8: CHALLENGES AND RISKS

Adopting a SIAM model requires an organizational transformation. The changes that are involved will affect people, processes, technology and the interfaces between them.

As with any organizational change, there will be challenges to face. These challenges can have a significant impact on the transition to a SIAM model and will require concerted effort to overcome.

Each challenge has associated risks, which need to be recorded, evaluated, managed and mitigated (where appropriate) using a risk management methodology. The impact of the challenge and associated risks will influence the amount of time and resources that will be used to address them.

The challenges and risks described here should be considered by any organization planning to adopt SIAM. They may not all be relevant, but can provide useful input for SIAM planning.

8.1 Challenge: Building the business case

Organizations must be clear about their business case for SIAM. This should include the expected benefits and costs.

It is not always possible to have a complete picture during the Discovery & Strategy stage of the roadmap, as some of the detail may not be known until the Plan & Build stage. However, it is usual to create an outline business case before starting a SIAM implementation that will be developed throughout the SIAM roadmap into a full business case.

The business case should include the drivers that apply to the organization, drawn from the five SIAM driver groups (documented in **section 1.5.2**):

- Service satisfaction
- Service and sourcing landscape
- Operational efficiencies
- External drivers
- Commercial drivers

The business case also needs to articulate the benefits that the organization expects to achieve by adopting a SIAM model. These could include, for example:

- Mitigating the risk of procuring services from a single provider by leveraging best-of-breed services from several providers
- Improving its capability to add and remove service providers
- Improving the quality of service
- Increasing the value derived from IT services

These benefits will only be achieved though clear objectives, robust planning, and effective management.

8.1.1 Which parties will this challenge affect?

This challenge mainly applies to the customer that is creating the business case. It can also apply to an organization that intends to be an external service integrator, as it will need to be able to justify the cost of its services.

8.1.2 Which roadmap stage will this challenge affect?

This challenge starts early in the SIAM roadmap, during Discovery & Strategy, and continues all the way through.

At the end of the Discovery & Strategy stage, executive backing is required to approve the outline business case for SIAM, and to allocate resources to the next stage.

At the end of the Plan & Build stage, executive backing is required to authorize any procurements and allocate resources to the remaining stages. The business case will also be used during the Implement and Run & Improve stages to verify that the anticipated benefits are being realized.

8.1.3 Associated risks

Without a strong business case, there are several risks, including:

- The customer organization's executives do not approve the transition to SIAM
- The customer organization's executives approve the transition to SIAM, but do not allocate enough resources or provide sufficient support
- The customer organization starts the transformation process without a clear picture of the benefits it expects to achieve; this will make it difficult to verify if the transition to SIAM has been successful
- The success of the program cannot be measured because anticipated benefits have not been clearly defined
- The costs of the transition to SIAM are understated, so there may not be enough budget available to complete the transition

8.1.4 Potential mitigation

These risks can be mitigated by:

- Allocating skilled resources to build the business case
- Executing all the activities in the Discovery & Strategy and Plan & Build stages
- Linking the strategy for SIAM to the customer organization's high-level strategy and objectives
- Identifying and addressing each of the appropriate drivers for the SIAM transformation
- Adding as much detail as possible and refining the business case as the roadmap proceeds
- Identifying any current contracts that are inefficient
- Identifying contracts that are providing good value and are a good cultural fit
- Using industry data/benchmarks where available to show the benefits of SIAM in other organizations
- Including the proposed SIAM structure and SIAM model
- Documenting the expected benefits

8.2 Challenge: Level of control and ownership

During the Discovery & Strategy stage of the roadmap, the customer organization needs to consider how it will balance the level of control it wants to have over service provision, processes, tools and data against the benefits it will obtain from delegating them to a service integrator. This decision is then confirmed in the Plan & Build stage.

This level of control also depends on the trust within the environment. Trust between all parties is essential in SIAM ecosystems. A lack of trust can manifest itself as duplication of roles and activities, such as the customer continually checking what the service integrator has done. The customer organization might be unable to let go of activities it used to perform.

It can also result in micro-management, for example the service integrator reviewing every aspect of every change from the service providers.

All of this will increase cost, leading to savings and efficiencies not being realized. It can also cause confusion, inconsistency, poor relationships, and a lack of collaboration.

8.2.1 Which parties will this challenge affect?

This challenge mainly applies to the customer organization while it decides on its preferred SIAM structure and model, and sets policies related to roles, responsibilities, data and tooling.

If this challenge is not resolved, it can make the definition of the SIAM model, and the role of the service integrator and service providers, more challenging because responsibilities and accountabilities are unclear.

Micro-management or a lack of trust embedded within the model can affect the customer organization, service integrator and service providers.

8.2.2 Which roadmap stage will this challenge affect?

The level of control and ownership needs to be decided at a high level during Discovery & Strategy, and more detail added during Plan & Build.

This challenge will usually be identified after SIAM has become business as usual, so in the Implement and Run & Improve roadmap stages.

8.2.3 Associated risks

If the level of control and ownership is not clearly defined, associated risks include:

- If the customer is not prepared to relinquish ownership of service activities and processes, it may not be possible to realize the anticipated benefits from SIAM, as the service integrator may be unable to perform its role.
- The organization is larger than needed as process and service activities are duplicated by the customer and the service integrator.
- The customer organization wastes time and resources micro-managing and checking the work of the service integrator.
- The service integrator wastes time and resources providing extra, unnecessary customer reports.

- The service integrator wastes time and resources micro-managing and checking the work of the service providers.
- The service providers continue to interact directly with the customer, because they see the customer does not value the service integrator (or they do not trust the service integrator.
- If the customer relinquishes all control and accountability, the service integrator might not have enough strategic direction to allow it to carry out its role.

8.2.4 Potential mitigation

These risks can be mitigated by:

- Defining a clear vision and selecting an appropriate SIAM structure and SIAM model during the Discovery & Strategy, and Plan & Build stages of the roadmap.
- Ensuring that the customer organization understands the difference between governance and management, so it is clear what activities it needs to monitor, and what it needs to do. This will form part of the governance framework.
- Careful design of the SIAM model in the Plan & Build stage, particularly roles, responsibilities and governance framework.
- Implementing clear policies for data, tooling and processes.
- Defining ownership of processes, tools, data, information and knowledge.
- Adopting a phased approach to the implementation of SIAM to allow the customer to develop trust in the service integrator and test the level of control (not too much, not too little ... just right).
- Having regular communication and a culture of improvement to identify and discuss micro-management and duplication of effort.

Establishing effective structural elements to support relationships and communication, and build trust.

8.3 Challenge: Commercial challenges

Commercial challenges relate to how the SIAM model is established and the structure that is chosen. The customer, service integrator and service providers all need to feel they are getting what they expect and are being treated fairly.

If a customer organization does not have mature SIAM capabilities, the commercial agreements it puts in place may not be appropriate.

For existing service providers, there may be challenges associated with legacy contracts. The two main challenges are:

- **Not fit for purpose:** some legacy contracts might still be in place after the SIAM implementation. The contractual requirements in the legacy contract with the service provider are unlikely to align with the new SIAM model
- **Expiry:** continuity of service may be compromised if legacy service provider contracts expire before the implementation of new service provider contracts

It is important to recognize that service providers that are not going to be part of the future operating model may be challenging to deal with.

8.3.1 Which parties will this challenge affect?

All the parties in the SIAM ecosystem can be affected by this challenge:

- The customer needs to feel they are getting value for money
- Externally sourced service integrators and all service providers need to be profitable and not incur penalties they see as unfair
- The service integrator and the customer need to have an appropriate commercial framework to govern and incentivize the service providers

8.3.2 Which roadmap stage will this challenge affect?

This challenge will span the entire roadmap. Contracts that may not be fit for purpose should be identified during the Discovery & Strategy roadmap stage. Commercial decisions will also be made during Discovery & Strategy, and then detail will be added and contracts defined during Plan & Build.

The effects will need to be monitored during Implement and Run & Improve activities identified where necessary.

Contract expiry will affect the Plan & Build stage, and can also affect the Implement and Run & Improve stages.

8.3.3 Associated risks

Commercial risks include:

- Unrealistic targets and service levels for service providers may result in their withdrawing from the ecosystem.
- Lack of clearly defined boundaries between service providers make it challenging to allocate responsibility for service failures.
- The service integrator is managing the service providers from a SIAM perspective but does not have any direct contracts with them; unless the right level of empowerment is in place, the service integrator may not be effective.
- The service providers impose their own contracts that have targets that do not align with end-to-end service requirements (for example, when the service provider is a very large organization, it may have a standard set of service levels.
- Increased service integrator workload, when unexpired legacy contracts need to be integrated into the SIAM model.
- A gap in service if a legacy contract expires before a new SIAM-based contract is in place.
- Additional customer costs for extensions to existing contracts during the transition to SIAM, or for early release from an existing contract.

8.3.4 Potential mitigation

Commercial risks can be mitigated by:

- Getting the right skills and experience involved during contractual negotiations
- Defining service boundaries and service interactions
- Including in service provider contracts that the service integrator is the managing agent of the customer, with devolved authority for managing delivery against contracts
- Making sure targets and service levels flow down and are apportioned across service providers
- Ensuring that penalties and service credits can be calculated correctly
- Having clear and unambiguous contracts
- Scheduling regular reviews to assess if contracts are performing as they should

Risks associated with contracts considered not fit for purpose or expiring too early can be mitigated by:

- Understanding to which contracts this relates and creating a timetable to project how long the risk will exist for
- Developing a roadmap for the transition to SIAM that aligns with existing expiry dates as far as possible
- Sharing the new SIAM vision with the existing service providers
- Renegotiating/amending contracts where possible; it is possible that requirements, SLAs, measurements or end dates could be changed
- Investigating the cost of termination

8.4 Challenge: Security

Implementing a SIAM model requires sharing of data and information about services across multiple service providers. Security needs to be embedded in every layer, through roles, responsibilities, communication and reporting.

The customer organization needs to be clear about what data and information exists in the ecosystem, where it is, and how it will be managed and secured.

8.4.1 Which parties will this challenge affect?

This challenge affects the customer, service integrator and service providers; each party has a responsibility for the overall security of the service.

8.4.2 Which roadmap stage will this challenge affect?

If security-related roles and activities are not clearly defined during Plan & Build, the impact will be felt in later roadmap stages.

In a worst-case scenario, a security incident during 'Run' might take longer to discover because no one party is responsible for detecting it. The response could also be slow because the service providers do not have clarity on individual responsibilities.

8.4.3 Associated risks

Risks associated with security include:

- A lack of understanding of the customer organization's legislative and regulatory responsibilities, and a lack of education for the service integrator and service providers to make them aware of these.
- A lack of understanding of the criticality of information, and no agreed approach to managing information.
- Inability to map data flows and the end-to-end service, to identify what is in scope for security
- Security roles and responsibilities not mapped and allocated.
- Process inadequacies, including a lack of access management for service providers to ensure they can only access what is necessary.
- Ineffective data segregation, particularly in relation to a service provider's commercially sensitive data that should not be visible to other service providers.
- If roles are not clear, security tasks might be duplicated, leading to wasted effort, or not managed, leading to service unavailability and security breaches.

8.4.4 Potential mitigation

These risks can be mitigated by:

- Having a clear security strategy and supporting policies that are cascaded to all service providers via the service integrator
- Using other practices like COBIT and OBASHI to help identify information assets and data flows
- Designing and implementing end-to-end security management
- Implementing effective processes such as access management
- Identifying and completing security activities when adding and removing service providers; service providers being added need enough access to be effective, and service providers that are being removed need to have access terminated
- Creating a schedule for audits and testing
- Encouraging a culture of openness so service providers are confident to share information about a breach
- Establishing a process forum for security

8.5 Challenge: Cultural fit and behaviors

Different service providers will have different corporate cultures, which all need to work within the SIAM ecosystem.

Service providers need to work together to meet customer outcomes, often with organizations with which they are in competition in the broader marketplace.

Existing service providers might not be willing to change to adapt to the SIAM model. When a major organizational change happens, it is easy and tempting for staff to revert to old ways of working with which they are more familiar.

This might mean that the intended value of the SIAM implementation is not realized, because the implementation does not become business as usual or an accepted way of working. An effective SIAM ecosystem relies on much more than just contractual agreements. It also relies on good relationships between the customer, service integrator and service providers.

New service providers also need to be a good cultural fit and display the required behaviors.

8.5.1 Which parties will this challenge affect?

This challenge affects the customer, service integrator and service providers; each party has a role to play in cultural change and should adopt required behaviors to make the SIAM model successful.

8.5.2 Which roadmap stage will this challenge affect?

This challenge needs to be addressed initially in Plan & Build. The issues will increase during the Implement stage, and may worsen during Run & Improve.

In the Implement stage, SIAM is often the new way of working and all parties need to work together to implement the SIAM model. In Run & Improve, it needs to become business as usual. Behaviors need to be reviewed continually, and revisited if key staff change or a new service provider is added.

8.5.3 Associated risks

Potential risks associated with cultural fit include:

- Service provider staff circumventing the service integrator to talk directly to the customer, and vice versa
- One or more service providers not engaging fully
- Frustration for all parties if a service provider says one thing and does another
- Service providers not working well together
- Service providers not interacting with end-to-end processes and procedures
- The service integrator being unable to fulfil its role because the service providers are not working together effectively
- The service integrator being perceived as biased
- The customer or service integrator acting in a dictatorial way and not having good relationships with the service providers
- The customer and service integrator not presenting a united front
- Cultural issues leading to SIAM benefits not being delivered to the customer organization

8.5.4 Potential mitigation

These risks can be mitigated by:

- Being aware of the risk of cultural mismatch, and planning to identify it and intervene where required
- Assessing cultural fit during procurement and selecting service providers that will be a good cultural fit
- Regular behavior reviews and audits
- Rewarding good behaviors

- Encouraging a culture of collaboration
- Using collaboration agreements (see **section 7.2.4.2**)
- Demonstrating correct behavior at the customer and service integrator level, presenting a united front to service providers
- Continual reinforcement of correct behavior at all levels
- Ongoing training and awareness for staff
- Establishing SIAM structural elements (boards, forums and working groups) to build relationships and reinforce culture
- Providing regular communication to build relationships, based on a communication plan that identifies relevant stakeholder groups and describes a communication strategy for each of them
- The customer and service integrator being realistic about what can be achieved by working with service providers, rather than punishing them

8.6 Challenge: Measuring success

To show that SIAM is delivering value, it must be measured. Developing an end-to-end performance management and reporting framework that spans multiple service providers can be a significant challenge.

8.6.1 Which parties will this challenge affect?

This challenge will affect the customer if it is unable to validate whether SIAM is delivering value and services are performing, and the service integrator that has the task of building the end-to-end reports.

8.6.2 Which roadmap stage will this challenge affect?

This challenge will usually happen during Run & Improve, when the customer tries to measure the effectiveness of SIAM in the business-as-usual environment.

The measures should be defined during Plan & Build, linked to the original drivers for SIAM identified in Discovery & Strategy. Measurements will need to evolve when improvement activities take place.

8.6.3 Associated risks

Risks associated with measuring success include:

- Measures not aligned with the anticipated benefits from the business case
- Not measuring and reporting on the right things
- Measuring too much, which wastes resources and can obscure important information
- Not measuring enough to identify the required information
- Being unable to measure services from end to end

8.6.4 Potential mitigation

These risks can be mitigated by:

- Creating an effective performance management and reporting framework
- Clearly defining who needs to measure what, when, how and why
- Regularly reviewing reports to confirm they are still fit for purpose
- Using a mix of qualitative and quantitative measures

APPENDIX A: GLOSSARY OF TERMS

This glossary defines the terms used in this book. This includes the specific SIAM definitions for common terms such as 'board'.

Aggregation	Also referred to as service aggregation. Bringing together components and elements to create a group (or service).
Board	Boards perform governance in the SIAM ecosystem. They are formal decision-making bodies, and are accountable for the decisions that they take. Boards are a type of structural element.
Business as usual (BAU)	The normal state of something.
Business case	Outlines a proposed course of action, its potential costs and benefits. Supports decision-making.
Capability	*"The power or ability to do something."*[29]
Cloud services	Services that are provided over the internet, including Software as a Service (SaaS), Infrastructure as a Service (IaaS) and Platform as a Service (PaaS). Often treated as a commodity service.
COBIT®	COBIT® (Control Objectives for Information and Related Technologies) is a framework for IT governance and management created by ISACA.
Code of conduct	A code of conduct (or 'rules of the club') document is not a contractual agreement. It provides high-level guidance for how the parties in the SIAM ecosystem will work together.
Collaboration agreement	A collaboration agreement helps to create a culture based on working together to deliver shared outcomes, without continual reference back to contracts.

---

[29] *www.lexico.com/definition/capability.*

Commodity service	A service that can easily be replaced; for example, internet hosting is often a commodity service.
Contract	An agreement between two legal entities. SIAM contracts are often shorter in duration than traditional outsourcing contracts, and have targets to drive collaborative behavior and innovation.
Customer (organization)	The customer organization is the end client that is making the transition to SIAM as part of its operating model. It commissions the SIAM ecosystem.
Disaggregation	Splitting a group into component parts.
Ecosystem	The SIAM ecosystem includes three layers: customer organization (including retained capabilities), service integrator and service provider(s).
Enterprise architecture	A definition of the structure and operation of an organization. It maps the current state and can be used to support planning for desired future states.
Enterprise service bus	A type of 'middleware' that provides services to link more complex architectures.
External service provider	An external service provider is an organization that provides services and is not part of the customer organization. It is a separate legal entity.
Externally sourced service integrator	Type of SIAM structure: the customer appoints an external organization to take the role and provide the capabilities of the service integrator.
Function	*"An organizational entity, typically characterized by a special area of knowledge or experience."*[30]
Governance	Governance refers to the rules, policies, processes (and in some cases, legislation) by which businesses are operated, regulated and controlled. There may be many layers of governance within a business from enterprise, corporate and IT. In a SIAM ecosystem, governance refers to the definition and application of policies and standards. These define and

---

[30] IT Process Wiki, *https://wiki.en.it-processmaps.com/index.php/ITIL_Functions*.

	ensure the required levels of authority, decision-making and accountability.
Governance framework	Within a SIAM ecosystem, allows the customer organization to exercise and maintain authority over the ecosystem. It includes corporate governance requirements, controls to be retained by the customer, governance structural elements, segregation of duties, and risk, performance, contract and dispute management approaches.
Governance model	Designed based on the governance framework and roles and responsibilities. Includes scope, accountabilities, responsibilities, meeting formats and frequencies, inputs, outputs, hierarchy, terms of reference and related policies.
Hybrid service integrator	Type of SIAM structure: the customer collaborates with an external organization to take the role of service integrator and provide the service integrator capability.
Infrastructure as a Service (IaaS)	A type of cloud service that allows customers to access virtualized computing resources.
Insourcing	Sourcing from within the organization.
Intelligent client function	See retained capabilities.
Internal service provider	An internal service provider is a team or department that is part of the customer organization. Its performance is typically managed using internal agreements and targets.
Internally sourced service integrator	Type of SIAM structure: the customer organization takes the role of service integrator, providing the service integration capability.
ITIL®	ITIL® is the most widely accepted approach to IT service management in the world, and is a registered trademark of AXELOS Limited.
Key performance indicator (KPI)	A metric used to measure performance. KPIs are defined for services, processes and business objectives.

Layers (SIAM layers)	There are three layers in the SIAM ecosystem: customer organization (including retained capabilities), service integrator and service provider(s).
Lead supplier service integrator	Type of SIAM structure: the role of service integrator is taken by an external organization that is also an external service provider.
Man-marking	An undesirable and wasteful type of micro-management, where the customer checks the work of the service integrator constantly.
Management methodology	A management methodology describes methods, rules and principles associated with a discipline.
Microsoft Operations Framework (MOF)	A guide for IT professionals that describes how to create, implement and manage services.
Model (SIAM model)	A customer organization develops its SIAM model based on the practices, processes, functions, roles and structural elements described within the SIAM methodology. Its model will be based on the layers in the SIAM ecosystem.
Multi-sourcing	Sourcing of goods or services from more than one supplier.
Multi-sourcing integration (MSI)	May be used as an acronym for SIAM.
Open Systems Interconnection (OSI)	A reference model for how applications communicate over a network.
Operational-level agreement (OLA)	Within the SIAM context, OLAs are created between parties (for instance, the service integrator and a service provider) to break down end-to-end service targets into detail and individual responsibilities.
Organizational change management	The process used to manage changes to business processes, organizational structures and cultural changes within an organization.
Outsourcing	Procuring goods or services from an external organization.

Performance management and reporting framework	The performance management and reporting framework for SIAM addresses measuring and reporting on a range of items, including: • Key performance indicators • Performance of processes and process models • Achievement of service level targets • System and service performance • Adherence to contractual and non-contractual responsibilities • Collaboration • Customer satisfaction
Platform as a Service (PaaS)	A type of cloud service that allows customers to use virtual platforms for their application development and management. This removes the need for them to build their own infrastructure.
Practice	The actual application or use of an idea, belief or method, as opposed to theories relating to it.[31]
Prime vendor	A sourcing approach where the service provider subcontracts to other service providers to deliver the service, and the customer only has a contractual relationship with the prime vendor.
Process	A documented, repeatable approach to carrying out a series of tasks or activities.
Process forum	Process forums are aligned to specific processes or practices. Their members work together on proactive development, innovations and improvements. Forums will convene regularly, for as long as the SIAM model is in place. Process forums are a type of structural element.
Process manager	Responsible for process execution.
Process model	Describes the purpose and outcomes for a process, as well as activities, inputs, outputs, interactions, controls, measures, and supporting policies and templates.

---

[31] *www.lexico.com/definition/practice*.

Process owner	A process owner is accountable for end-to-end process design and process performance.
Program management	The process responsible for managing groups of projects to deliver a unified goal.
Project management	A process that provides a repeatable approach to deliver successful projects.
RACI	RACI is an acronym that stands for Responsible, Accountable, Consulted and Informed. These are the four principal 'involvements' that can be assigned to an activity and a role. A RACI chart is a matrix of all the activities or decision-making authorities undertaken in an organization set against all the people or roles.
Request for information (RFI)	A business process used to compare suppliers, by collecting information about them and their capabilities.
Request for proposal (RFP)	A business process used to allow suppliers to bid for a piece of work or project.
Retained capability/ capabilities	The customer organization will include some retained capabilities. The retained capabilities are the functions that are responsible for strategic, architectural, business engagement and corporate governance activities. The service integrator is independent from the retained capabilities, even if it is sourced internally. Service integration is not a retained capability. Retained capabilities are sometimes referred to as the 'intelligent client function'.
Roadmap	The SIAM roadmap has four stages: Discovery & Strategy, Design & Build, Implement, Run & Improve.
Separation of duties/concerns	An internal control used to prevent errors or fraud, separation of duties defines what each role is authorized to do and when more than one person must be involved in a task. For example, a developer might not be permitted to test and approve their own code.
Service	A system that meets a need, for example email is an 'IT service' that facilitates communication.

Service boundaries	A definition of what parts make up a service (what is 'inside the boundary'), often used in technical architecture documents.
Service consumer	The organization directly using the service.
Service integration (SI)	May be used as an acronym for SIAM.
Service integration and management (SIAM)	Service integration and management (SIAM) is a management methodology that can be applied in an environment that includes services sourced from a number of service providers. Sometimes referred to as SI&M.
Service integrator	A single, logical entity held accountable for the end-to-end delivery of services and the business value that the customer receives. The service integrator is accountable for end-to-end service governance, management, integration, assurance and coordination.
Service integrator layer	The service integrator layer of the SIAM ecosystem is where end-to-end service governance, management, integration, assurance and coordination is performed.
Service management	The management practices and capabilities that an organization uses to provide services to consumers.
Service management and integration (SMAI)	May be used as an acronym for SIAM.
Service management integration (SMI)	May be used as an acronym for SIAM.
Service manager	Responsible for service delivery for one or more services.
Service model	A way of modelling the hierarchy of services, including services that are directly consumed by the customer organization and underpinning services and dependencies.
Service orchestration	Service orchestration is the term used to define the end-to-end view of service activities and establishing the standards for inputs and outputs to the end-to-end process. This includes defining control mechanisms while

	still allowing service providers to define the mechanisms of fulfilment and the freedom to pursue internal processes.
Service outcomes	A definition of what a service is meant to achieve or deliver.
Service owner	A role that is accountable for the end-to-end performance of a service.
Service provider	Within a SIAM ecosystem, there are multiple service providers. Each service provider is responsible for the delivery of one or more services, or service elements, to the customer. It is responsible for managing the products and technology used to deliver its contracted or agreed services, and operating its own processes. They can be internal or external to the customer organization. Historically referred to as towers, and may also be referred to as vendors or suppliers.
Service provider category	Service providers can be categorized as strategic, tactical or commodity.
Shadow IT	Shadow IT describes IT services and systems commissioned by business departments, without the knowledge of the IT department (sometimes referred to as 'stealth IT').
SIAM model	See 'Model'.
SIAM structures	The four structures describe how the service integrator is sourced: internally, externally, from a lead supplier or as a hybrid.
Software as a Service (SaaS)	A cloud service where software is paid for monthly as a subscription rather than purchased as a one-time payment.
Sourcing	The procurement approach an organization adopts; for example, sourcing services internally or externally. Adopting SIAM will affect how an organization sources services and the types of contracts it puts in place with service providers.
Structural element	Structural elements are teams that have members from different organizations and different SIAM layers. They include boards, process forums and working groups.
Supplier	An organization from which the customer receives goods or services.

Tooling strategy	Defines what tools will be used, who will own them and how they will support the flow of data and information between the SIAM layers.
Tower	See 'Service provider'.
Watermelon effect (Watermelon reporting)	The watermelon effect occurs when a report is 'green on the outside, red on the inside'. The service provider(s) meet individual targets, but the end-to-end service is not meeting the customer's requirements.
Working group	Working groups are convened to address specific issues or projects. They are typically formed on a reactive ad hoc or fixed-term basis. They can include staff from different organizations and different specialist areas. Working groups are a structural element.

List of acronyms

This list expands the acronyms used in this document.

ADKAR	Awareness, desire, knowledge, ability and reinforcement
Agile SM	Agile Service Management
BAU	Business as usual
BiSL	Business Information Services Library
BoK	Body of Knowledge
CALMS	Culture, Automation, Lean, Measurement, Sharing
CFO	Chief Financial Officer
CIO	Chief Information Officer
CMM(I)	Capability Maturity Model (Integration)
COBIT®	Control Objectives for Information and Related Technologies
CSO	Chief Security Officer

CTO	Chief Technical Officer
EXIN	Examination Institute for Information Science
HDI	Help Desk Institute
IaaS	Infrastructure as a Service
IEC	International Electrotechnical Commission
IFDC	International Foundation for Digital Competences
ISACA	Information Systems Audit and Control Association
ISO	International Organization for Standardization
IT	Information technology
ITIL®	Information Technology Infrastructure Library
ITO	IT outsourcer (or organization)
ITSM	IT service management
itSMF	Information Technology Service Management Forum
KPI	Key performance indicator
LAN	Local area network
MSI	Multi-sourcing integration
MVP	Minimum viable process (or product)
OBASHI	Ownership, business processes, applications, systems, hardware and infrastructure
OLA	Operational-level agreement
OSI	Open Systems Interconnection

PaaS	Platform as a Service
RACI	Responsible, accountable, consulted and informed
RFI	Request for information
RFP	Request for proposal
SaaS	Software as a Service
SI	Service integration
SIAM	Service integration and management
SLA	Service level agreement
SMAI	Service management and integration
SMI	Service management integration
SMS	Short message service (telephony) Service management system (ISO)
SVC	Service Value Chain
SVS	Service Value System
TOGAF	The Open Group Architecture Framework
UK	United Kingdom
VeriSM	Value-driven, Evolving, Responsive, Integrated, Service Management
VVI	Voice and VIdeo
WAN	Wide area network

APPENDIX B: THE SIAM™ PROCESS GUIDES

1. What is a process?

A process is "a documented, repeatable approach to carrying out a series of tasks or activities".

Most business activities involve repeated tasks; for example, taking a phone call from a customer, raising an invoice or managing a complaint.

Documenting a process for a repeated task has several benefits:

- It allows the organization to define its preferred approach to managing the task
- The task will be carried out consistently
- It avoids staff wasting time recreating an approach each time the task is carried out
- New staff can be trained quickly to carry out a process
- It can be measured and assessed
- It can be used as a baseline for improvement

A process takes one or more inputs, performs activities on them and transforms them into one or more outputs.

A process description document will normally include:

- The purpose and objectives of the process
- The trigger for starting the process
- Process activities or steps
- Roles and responsibilities, including a RACI model
- Metrics for the process, including service levels, targets and key performance indicators
- Process inputs and outputs
- Escalation paths
- Associated toolsets
- Data and information requirements

Every process should have an owner. The owner is the single, accountable role that ensures the process is defined, executed and reviewed correctly. In larger organizations, process manager roles might also be part of the organizational structure; these roles are responsible for the execution of process activities.

For example, the process owner for change management might be the organization's change manager, who could be supported by a number of change analysts. They, in turn, would be fulfilling process manager-type roles.

Processes are part of an organization's SIAM model.

This document describes some common processes at a high level and includes SIAM considerations to help organizations adapt processes within a SIAM ecosystem.

This is not an exhaustive list of processes used within SIAM ecosystems; neither is it an in-depth process guide for commonly used service management processes that are fully described in other management practices, frameworks and standards like ISO/IEC 20000.

2. Processes and the SIAM ecosystem

SIAM itself is not a process; however, to operate effectively, it relies on a number of processes. Within a SIAM ecosystem, processes are likely to be executed:

- Across different organizations in the same SIAM layer
- Across organizations in different SIAM layers

Processes need to be allocated to the appropriate layers in the SIAM model. This allocation may be different for each implementation of SIAM.

Many of the processes used within a SIAM ecosystem are processes familiar from other management practices, for example change management and business relationship management.

Within a SIAM model, these processes require adaptation and augmentation to support integration and coordination between the parties involved. They also require alignment with other parts of the SIAM model, including:

- SIAM practices
- SIAM layers
- Governance model
- Structural elements

The execution of many processes will span multiple layers and involve multiple parties. For example, the customer organization and service integrator can both carry out elements of supplier management; the service integrator and service providers will each have responsibilities in the end-to-end change management process.

Each service provider might carry out individual process steps in a different way, but as part of an overall integrated process model. Process models are therefore important SIAM artefacts; local processes and work instructions are likely to remain within the domain of the individual organization that performs the activities.

Each party in a SIAM ecosystem should adapt and augment its own processes to integrate with the relevant process models, as part of the overall SIAM model.

The detail of the process models, and the allocation of activities to the different layers in the SIAM structure, will vary for each implementation of SIAM. See the **SIAM Foundation Body of Knowledge, <u>section 2</u>** for more information on process models and how to design a SIAM model.

As each SIAM model is different, this document cannot prescribe who will do what for each process. In all SIAM models, it is important to ensure that the roles and responsibilities, interfaces and dependencies of the customer, service integrator and service providers are mapped, defined clearly and understood by all.

2.1 Process guides

The process guides in this document provide a generic description for each process, plus an illustration of the considerations that should be made when designing and using the process in a SIAM ecosystem.

Each process guide includes:

- Process purpose
- SIAM considerations
- Generic process information:
    - Activities
    - Example roles
    - Example metrics
    - Example inputs and outputs

3. Common SIAM considerations

This section examines the considerations that are common for all processes in a SIAM ecosystem.

3.1 Complexity

In a SIAM ecosystem, processes can seem more complex owing to factors that include:

- Discrete layers having different accountabilities and responsibilities within the same process
- An increased number of parties involved in end-to-end process execution
- The need to integrate different processes from multiple organizations to support the end-to-end process
- The number of interactions between processes from different organizations

Complex processes are more difficult to understand and follow. Wherever possible, processes in a SIAM ecosystem should be designed to avoid complexity.

3.2 Who owns the end-to-end process?

Defining process ownership and levels of accountability and responsibility will also be important in a SIAM ecosystem. Common factors include:

- The customer is ultimately accountable for process outcomes, as it is the organization that commissions the SIAM ecosystem
- The service integrator is accountable for:
  - o The overall design of the process models, supporting policies and data and information standards. It must ensure that the design will deliver required outcomes
  - o Its own local processes and procedures
- The service providers are accountable for the design of their own local processes and procedures, ensuring that they comply with the process models, supporting policies and data and information standards provided by the service integrator

3.3 Toolset considerations

The toolset(s) that will support processes need to be defined as part of the SIAM model. The decision confirming which toolset is to be used, and who will own it, is made during the Plan & Build stage of the SIAM roadmap.

The outcome of these decisions is documented in the tooling strategy. The decisions can only be made once the SIAM model has been finalized.

If the customer owns the toolset, it will make it less challenging to change the service integrator. Alternatively, using a toolset owned by an external service integrator might offer an opportunity to access a 'best of breed' toolset.

3.4 Data and information considerations

3.4.1 Who owns the data?

This decision needs to take into consideration what happens if a service provider or a service integrator is replaced. The customer organization should aim to have ownership of, or guaranteed access to, any data that is necessary to operate the services, for example incident records.

3.4.2 Who owns the intellectual property on artefacts?

As part of normal service operation in a SIAM ecosystem, artefacts will be created, for example knowledge articles in the knowledge management repository.

Intellectual property rights for these artefacts need to be defined and agreed in contracts or service agreements. There will be commercial considerations to take into account, for example a service provider may be unwilling to share its articles with another organization.

3.4.3 Is data and information consistent?

The SIAM model should include standards for data and information and supporting policies. A data dictionary will ensure all parties use common standards.

For example, there should be a minimum dataset for incident records and a standard definition of incident priorities and severities.

3.4.4 How is access to shared data, information and tools controlled?

Policies and processes for access control need to be defined and managed, taking into account security considerations.

3.4.5 Who is responsible for process improvement?

All parties in the SIAM ecosystem are responsible for improving their own processes and for improving the end-to-end processes, facilitated by the service integrator.

The service integrator is responsible for ensuring that the processes from different service providers continue to work together within the overall process models.

The service integrator's process owners are accountable for end-to-end process improvement.

3.4.6 How will compliance and assurance be managed?

Compliance and assurance requirements should be included in contracts so that they can be enforced.

The service integrator is accountable for assurance of process outcomes across the end-to-end processes.

4. Process guide: Service portfolio management

4.1 Process purpose

The purpose of the service portfolio management process is to maintain information on all services, to provide the customer organization with a better insight into ongoing spend and support business decisions on future investment in products and services.

The process creates a single source of service information and tracks the status of planned, current and retired services.

4.2 SIAM considerations

Service portfolio management considerations in a SIAM environment include:

- It is not possible to make the transition to a SIAM model without a clear definition of all services, service providers, dependencies and relationships between services and service characteristics. Service portfolio management information is, therefore, critical to any SIAM implementation.
- The customer organization should own the service portfolio. Responsibility for execution of the service portfolio management process can be given to the customer's retained capabilities or delegated to the service integrator.
- The portfolio needs to be maintained with current information from all service providers, including potential new services arising from innovation opportunities. Service provider contracts need to include a requirement to provide this information.
- Data and information standards for portfolio records need to be agreed and consistent across all service providers.
- The service portfolio management process must be aligned with the processes for introducing and retiring new services and new service providers.

4.3 Generic process information

4.3.1 Activities

Service portfolio management activities can include:

- Creating a service portfolio
- Maintaining a service portfolio
- Reviewing a service portfolio

4.3.2 Example roles

Service portfolio management roles can include:

- Service portfolio manager

4.3.3 Example metrics

Service portfolio management metrics can include:

- The number of:

  o Planned services
  o Current services
  o Retired services
  o Portfolio opportunities
- Commercial viability of services

4.3.4 Example inputs and outputs

Service portfolio management inputs can include:

- Customer strategy and requirements
- Demand management data
- Service portfolio reviews
- Service catalogs
- Service contracts
- New and changed services

Service portfolio management outputs can include:

- Service portfolio
- Service portfolio reports
- Approved services
- Terminated services

5. Process guide: Monitoring and measuring

5.1 Process purpose

The purpose of the monitoring and measuring process is to:

- Monitor and measure systems and service delivery
- Monitor services against defined thresholds, creating alerts, identifying and predicting service affecting trends, and preventing service interruptions
- Measuring service utilization and performance

This process has relationships with other processes, including event management and service level management.

5.2 SIAM considerations

Monitoring and measuring considerations in a SIAM environment include:

- Assuring the ability of all service providers to monitor their services and underlying technical components
- The requirement for a data dictionary, data models, terminology, thresholds and reporting schedules that are consistent across the SIAM ecosystem
- Shared performance measures to enable end-to-end reporting

5.3 Generic process information

5.3.1 Activities

Monitoring and measuring activities can include:

- Service monitoring
- Threshold detection
- Incident detection
- Event creation
- Report creation
- Performance analysis
- Tuning

5.3.2 Example roles

Monitoring and measuring roles can include:

- Service level manager
- Service delivery manager
- Capacity manager
- Availability manager
- Event manager
- Performance manager

5.3.3 *Example metrics*

Monitoring and measuring metrics can include:

- Incidents related to capacity/availability issues
- Availability of services
- Performance of services
- Reports issued within schedule

5.3.4 *Example inputs and outputs*

Monitoring and measuring inputs can include:

- Contractual service levels
- Service thresholds
- Alerts
- Service provider data
- Reporting requirements, formats and frequencies

Monitoring and measuring outputs can include:

- Measurement reports
- Service measurements
- Service improvement opportunities
- Events
- Forecasts
- Change requests

6. Process guide: Event management

6.1 Process purpose

The purpose of the event management process is to identify events through the monitoring of technology components, systems and services, and, where appropriate, action is taken.

The process seeks to provide early detection – and even avoidance – of system and service outages, and increase service availability for users. It is closely related to monitoring and measuring, incident management and availability management.

6.2 SIAM considerations

Event management considerations in a SIAM environment include:

- The organizational design should include the function responsible for managing events. This could be a central function provided by the service integrator, a virtual function provided by all service providers or individual functions in each service provider.
- The rules for managing event thresholds should be defined in a policy that is consistent across all service providers; for example, at what point do repeated events concerning slow performance result in an incident being raised.
- Specific tools may be required to collate events from multiple service providers, correlate the data and apply rules to identify end-to-end issues.
- Targets for event diagnosis and resolution should be common across service providers.

6.3 Generic process information

6.3.1 Activities

Event management activities can include:

- Record an event (often automatically created by monitoring systems)
- Diagnose and evaluate the event
- Create an associated incident, if required, and assign to the incident management process
- Close the event
- Configure and tune event management tools

6.3.2 Example roles

Event management roles can include:

- Event manager
- Operations team
- Service desk

6.3.3 Example metrics

Event management metrics can include:

- Number of events, by type

- Accuracy of event information, by type
- Number of incidents avoided
- Number of failures resolved

6.3.4 Example inputs and outputs

Event management inputs can include:

- Auto-generated alerts
- User reports of system failures

6.3.5 Event management outputs can include:

- Event data
- Trend reports
- Input to related processes, including incident and problem management

7. Process guide: Request management

7.1 Process purpose

The purpose of the request management process is to manage the lifecycle of service requests from users. This may also be known as request fulfilment or request catalog management.

Service requests are a means of accessing standard services or service offerings from a service provider for which a predefined authorization and qualification process exists. Requests can be made in several ways, including contacting a service desk, sending an email or accessing a self-help portal.

Examples of requests include the provision of standard components, such as hardware or an application, to obtain information and advice or to log complaints or compliments regarding the services received.

The objective of the process is to provide efficient handling of all 'in scope' service requests.

7.2 SIAM considerations

Request management considerations in a SIAM environment include:

- Request management will typically be performed within each service provider, using mostly predefined and repeatable procedures:
  - o Fulfilling some requests may require the involvement of more than one service provider, requiring integration between the specific process of each service provider and service integrator.
  - o The service integrator's responsibilities include acting as a point of escalation for request management issues and ensuring that request management operates effectively across the full ecosystem.
- The service desk plays a key role in coordinating service requests with, and across, the various providers. Therefore, the service desk should be tightly integrated with this process.
- As requests are typically predefined and repeatable, automation should be leveraged as much as possible to support consistent, efficient and effective fulfilment.

7.3 Generic process information

7.3.1 Activities

Request management activities can include:

- Request logging and validation
- Request categorization
- Request prioritization
- Request authorization/approval
- Request routing
- Coordination of fulfilment activities
- Escalation
- Status tracking
- Request review

- Request closure
- Managing and maintaining a request catalog
- Creating new request processes

7.3.2 Example roles

Request management roles can include:

- Request (fulfilment) manager
- Service desk
- Financial manager
- Service catalog manager
- Service level manager
- Release manager
- Deployment manager
- Capacity manager
- Change manager
- Access manager
- Incident manager

7.3.3 Example metrics

Request management metrics can include:

- Request fulfilment timescales against agreed SLAs
- Breakdown of requests (by category)
- Requests resolved through automation
- Costs per type of request
- User satisfaction related to request fulfilment
- Size of request backlog

7.3.4 Example inputs and outputs

Request management inputs can include:

- Requests from various sources, such as phone calls, forms, web interfaces or email
- Request models/templates
- Authorization
- Request for change (RFC)
- Request for information
- Request for updates on status

Request management outputs can include:

- Authorized/rejected requests
- Request management status reports
- Fulfilled service requests

- Incidents (rerouted)
- RFCs/standard changes
- Asset/configuration updates
- Updated request records
- Closed service requests
- Cancelled service requests
- Request catalog
- New request types for consideration

8. Process guide: Incident management

8.1 Process purpose

The purpose of the incident management process is to record and manage service issues (known as incidents) that are interrupting the availability of a service. The process also manages events that are degrading – or could degrade – service performance.

The process seeks to restore service. This is often within an agreed timescale, dictated by the priority of the incident, based on its impact and the speed by which it needs to be resolved.

8.2 SIAM considerations

Incident management considerations in a SIAM environment include:

- The incident management process model needs to support prompt restoration of service. This includes routing incidents to potential resolvers as quickly as possible and with the minimum number of parties involved. The associated service desk model needs to support this.
- Data and information standards for incident records, incident transfer and supporting tooling must be defined, to support the effective referral of incidents between service providers.
- Incident priorities and severities should be defined consistently across all parties.
- Roles and responsibilities must be defined for coordinating incident investigations that involve multiple service providers.
- Targets for incident resolution need to recognize that incidents may be referred between service providers. The referrals will take time and each service provider will have its own agreed targets. The end-to-end process needs to make sure that customer targets are not breached, even if every service provider achieves its own target.
- There is a risk that service providers may refer incidents to another service provider to avoid breaching a resolution time service level.
- Incident management teams from different providers are likely to be in different geographical locations, creating challenges for collaboration on incidents.

8.3 Generic process information

8.3.1 Activities

Incident management activities can include:
- Incident reporting
- Incident detection
- Incident categorization and prioritization
- Record creation
- Incident investigation
- Incident resolution
- Confirmation of resolution
- Incident record updated and closed
- Incident trend analysis

8.3.2 *Example roles*

Incident management roles can include:

- Incident manager
- Service desk
- Major incident manager
- Technical staff

8.3.3 *Example metrics*

Incident management metrics can include:

- Number of incidents (overall, by service, by site, etc.)
- Number of incidents resolved at first point of contact
- Incidents that needed to be reopened
- Customer satisfaction with the incident management process
- Incidents that have been assigned incorrectly

8.3.4 *Example inputs and outputs*

Incident management inputs can include:

- Events
- User reports

Incident management outputs can include:

- Incident records
- Resolved incidents
- Incident reports
- Incident metrics

9. Process guide: Problem management

9.1 Process purpose

The purpose of the problem management process is to manage the lifecycle of a problem, which is defined as the unknown underlying cause of an incident. It is also responsible for preventing incidents and problems from occurring or recurring.

The problem management process has both reactive and proactive aspects. The reactive aspect is concerned with solving problems in response to one or more incidents within an agreed timescale and based on the priority of the problem. The proactive aspect is concerned with preventing incidents from occurring in the first place.

9.2 SIAM considerations

Problem management considerations in a SIAM environment include:

- Getting all parties to take part in problem management working groups and forums, including joint working to resolve problems that involve multiple service providers
- Coordinating problem investigation and resolution activities across multiple service providers
- Encouraging and facilitating the sharing of data and information on problems with other service providers
- Aligning targets for problem resolution across service providers
- Creating and using common terminology, data, and information standards and problem classifications across service providers

9.3 Generic process information

9.3.1 Activities

Problem management activities can include:

- Review of incident(s) reported or trend analysis of incident records
- Creating problem records
- Categorizing and prioritizing problem records
- Identifying and communicating workarounds
- Identifying and addressing the root cause of a problem
- Proactively identifying and addressing potential problems

9.3.2 Example roles

Problem management roles can include:

- Problem manager
- Technical teams

9.3.3 Example metrics

Problem management metrics can include:

- Problems recorded per month – proactive and reactive

- Number of in-progress problems
- Number of resolved problems
- Number of recurring incidents while a problem is being investigated

9.3.4 Example inputs and outputs

Problem management inputs can include:

- Incident records
- Configuration management information
- Change records
- Workarounds

Problem management outputs can include:

- Problem records
- Problem reviews
- Resolved problems
- Workarounds
- Change requests
- Service improvements
- Knowledge articles
- Reports

10. Process guide: Change and release management

10.1 Process purpose

The purpose of the change management process is to enable changes to be made to services with minimal amounts of disruption.

A release is a collection of one or more changes tested and deployed together. Release management ensures that the integrity of the live environment is protected and that the correct changes are deployed.

Together, the processes ensure that consistent methods are used to assess, approve and deploy changes.

10.2 SIAM considerations

Change and release management considerations in a SIAM environment include:

Change management:

- The scope of change management needs to be defined clearly. The process can encompass many areas, including:
  - o Technology
  - o Processes
  - o Policies
  - o Organizational structures
  - o The SIAM model
- Common standards should be developed for data and information and included in a change policy. These include, for example, types of change, approval levels and notice periods.
- The roles and parties involved in reviewing and approving changes must be clearly defined and should include all organizations that may be affected by the change.
- Having different reviewers and approvers for different types and classes of change. Who approves a change should depend on risk and impact and if the change is an emergency.
- Allowing service providers to approve their own proven low-risk, repeatable changes that do not affect other service providers.
- Leveraging automated testing and deployment techniques to reduce the level of manual review required and improve change success rates.

Release management:

- Release planning and implementation needs to consider all the affected service providers, and the customer organization. This includes coordinating and scheduling releases to avoid negative impact.
- Responsibilities for testing integration between services from different service providers should be defined.
- Defined approaches for remediation to minimize business impact should the release implementation fail.
- There should be a consistent format and method for communicating information about releases.

10.3 Generic process information

10.3.1 Activities

Change and release management activities can include:

- Analysis of proposed changes
- Approving changes
- Scheduling changes
- Communication
- Packaging of releases
- Scheduling releases
- Testing releases
- Implementation and deployment
- Reviewing successful deployment

10.3.2 Example roles

Change and release management roles can include:

- Change requestor
- Change manager
- Release manager
- Test manager
- Product owners
- Change advisory board attendees

10.3.3 Example metrics

Change and release management metrics can include:

- Changes per month
- Successful changes/releases
- Emergency changes
- Failed changes/releases
- Number of incidents caused by changes

10.3.4 Example inputs and outputs

Change and release management inputs can include:

- Change policy
- Release policy
- Requests for change
- Incident and problem data related to changes
- Service targets
- Test results
- Configuration information

- Change and release plans

Change and release management outputs can include:

- Approved/rejected changes
- Change schedules
- Change/release communications
- Release plans
- Service availability plans
- Change reviews

11. Process guide: Configuration management

11.1 Process purpose

The purpose of the configuration management process is to identify, record, maintain and assure data and information about configuration items (CIs).

A CI can be anything used to deliver or support the services, including:

- A service
- A software application or product
- A hardware component
- Documentation

The types of CIs in scope are tailored on a customer-by-customer basis. There can be many different types of CI.

CI details are often held in one or more configuration management database (CMDB). The aggregation of multiple CMDBs and other data sources is referred to as a configuration management system (CMS).

Configuration management records and maintains details of the relationships between CIs and documents how they interact and rely upon each other.

Configuration management has interfaces with other processes, including:

- Incident management, which registers incidents against CIs and uses CI information to identify existing incidents for the affected CI or recent changes that may have caused an incident
- Change and release management, which registers changes against CIs and uses configuration management data to assess the potential impact of changes and is updated through release deployment
- Problem management, which uses configuration management information to identify incident trends

11.2 SIAM considerations

Configuration management considerations in a SIAM environment include:

- The scope of the service integrator's CMDB must be clear, and should only contain data that the service integrator needs to fulfil its responsibilities
- Service provider contracts and agreements need to stipulate the configuration management data they are required to provide
- Each organization is responsible for maintaining its own CMDB, containing the data necessary to support delivery of its own services
- Service providers need to share a subset of the data in their CMDB with the service integrator and other service providers, to support delivery of the end-to-end service
- A policy should be defined to specify common classifications and record contents for any configuration data that needs to be shared across parties in the SIAM ecosystem

- The approach, toolset integration and access control for sharing CMDB data between different parties needs careful consideration
- Where CMDB data is shared, responsibility for maintaining shared items must be defined
- Responsibilities for assessing and improving data quality and CMDB accuracy should be defined

11.3 Generic process information

11.3.1 Activities

Configuration management activities can include:

- Design and implementation of CMDB(s)
- Gathering data to populate CMDB(s)
- Updating data based on triggers including change management inputs
- Audit of configuration management data
- Documentation and investigation of any data discrepancies
- Providing reports as required

11.3.2 Example roles

Configuration management roles can include:

- Configuration manager
- Configuration analyst

11.3.3 Example metrics

Configuration management metrics can include:

- Number of CIs, by service provider, type, status, etc.
- Number of CI to CI relationships, by service
- Number of CIs with incomplete or missing information
- CIs that are verified/unverified
- CIs discovered that are not contained in the CMDB
- CIs in the CMDB that should be detected by automated discovery tools but have not

11.3.4 Example inputs and outputs

Configuration management inputs can include:

- Data from discovery tools
- Data and information from physical checks
- Incident records
- Change records
- Build information from infrastructure teams
- Application information from development teams

Configuration management outputs can include:

- CMDB records
- Verification schedules
- Verification reports

12. Process guide: Service level management

12.1 Process purpose

The purpose of the service level management (SLM) process is to ensure that service performance meets agreed requirements. These requirements are set out as service level targets in a contract or service agreement.

SLM contributes to, reviews and validates the service level targets against service provider capability and planned service provision.

Following the implementation of services, SLM will review, report on and drive performance against the targets continually.

12.2 SIAM considerations

SLM considerations in a SIAM environment include:

- Service providers need to recognize that the service integrator is acting as the agent of the customer and work with it on SLM activities and reporting.
- The scope of SLM should be clearly defined. Its activities need to be distinct from those of:
  - Supplier management
  - Contract management
  - Performance management
  - Business relationship management

  even if performed in the same layer. The interfaces between these processes should be mapped.
- SLM needs to include thresholds to define when a breach of performance should be escalated to supplier management, so the process can apply remedies.
- The SIAM model needs to reflect any service level targets that may have been agreed before the service integrator was appointed.
- The scope of the contracted services, and any dependencies on services from other service providers, must be clearly defined.
- An approach must be established to manage the situation where the failure of a service provider to meet its targets is due to another service provider's actions.
- The service integrator will need information to verify the service providers' performance reports. This may need to be sourced from other service providers and from service consumers.
- It can be challenging to produce consolidated reports unless the service level targets of all service providers are aligned. For example: a common definition and calculation of 'availability' and reports covering the same time periods.
- Consideration should be given to including internal service providers within the scope of SLM.

12.3 Generic process information

12.3.1 Activities

SLM activities can include:

- Tracking performance against service level targets

- Validating service reports from service providers
- Producing and publishing reports of service achievements against service levels and of trends
- Reviewing performance data to identify improvement opportunities
- Reviewing service level targets for ongoing alignment with business requirements

12.3.2 Example roles

SLM roles can include:

- Service level manager
- Reporting analyst

12.3.3 Example metrics

SLM metrics can include:

- Customer perception of the services
- Service level achievement against targets

SLM metrics are often trended on a monthly, quarterly and annual basis. This can highlight areas for improvement and successes.

12.3.4 Example inputs and outputs

SLM inputs can include:

- Contracts
- Service targets
- Service provider capabilities
- Service performance data
- Customer feedback

SLM outputs can include:

- Service level reports
- Trend analysis
- Service improvement opportunities

13. Process guide: Supplier management

13.1 Process purpose

The purpose of the supplier management process is to define the supplier management policy and strategy, establish a management framework, and identify and manage service providers, to deliver value for money to the customer.

The process manages supplier performance, in conjunction with service level management and contract management.

13.2 SIAM considerations

The 'suppliers' in a SIAM ecosystem are referred to as service providers.

Supplier management considerations in a SIAM environment include:

- Effective supplier management is critical to the success of any SIAM implementation. Performance issues with one service provider can affect others, as well as affecting the end-to-end service.
- Supplier management is normally executed by the service integrator, acting on behalf of the customer.
- Supplier management should be clearly defined as separate from contract management and service level management, even if performed in the same layer. The interfaces between these processes should be clear.
- This process should manage service provider performance escalations received from the service level management process.
- A supplier management policy should be created that is appropriate for, and fair to, different types and sizes of service providers.
- The execution of the process should not favor one service provider over others. This can be a challenge if the service integrator is also a service provider or where some service providers are internal.
- There should be a clear definition for when the supplier management process can apply remedies and for when a breach of performance becomes a breach of contract that should be escalated to contract management.
- A mechanism should be developed to apportion remedies for failure to meet service level targets where multiple service providers contributed to the failure.
- Non-financial incentives can be as effective as financial remedies to drive appropriate service provider behavior.
- Supplier forums can assist in creating a collaborative culture.

13.3 Generic process information

13.3.1 Activities

Supplier management activities can include:

- Plan, produce and implement a supplier management policy and process

- Enforce the policy
- Design and implement a supplier management framework
- Apply remedies for failure to meet service level targets
- Identify and manage nonconformity to the policy and process
- Escalate to contract management as required

13.3.2 Example roles

Supplier management roles can include:

- Supplier manager
- Account manager
- Procurement manager
- Contract manager
- Service provider service manager

13.3.3 Example metrics

Supplier management metrics can include:

- Number of suppliers managed in accordance with the policy
- Supplier performance aligned to committed performance targets
- Reduction of service failures
- Accuracy of service reporting and conformity to service level agreements

13.3.4 Example inputs and outputs

Supplier management inputs can include:

- Business policy requirements
- Contracts
- Audit reports
- Regulatory and industry standards
- Previous breaches and achievements
- Customer and supplier requirements
- Planned changes
- Project plans and risk logs

Supplier management outputs can include:

- Supplier conformity reports
- Planned improvements and remediation activities
- Training needs

14. Process guide: Contract management

14.1 Process purpose

The purpose of the contract management process is to:

- Evaluate proposals from prospective service providers
- Negotiate and finalize contracts with service providers
- Verify if contractual requirements are being met, and trigger contractual remediation if required
- Assess if contracts are still relevant and advise on updates or termination if no longer required

14.2 SIAM considerations

Contract management considerations in a SIAM environment include:

- The customer is always accountable for contract management; it holds the contracts with the service providers. Some organizations delegate responsibility for execution of some activities to an external service integrator or use them as an advisor.
- Contract management should be clearly defined as separate from supplier management and service level management, even if performed in the same layer. The interfaces between these processes should be clear.
- A SIAM ecosystem requires appropriate contracts to avoid vendor lock-in, and provide for shared goals, shared risk and reward, end-to-end service levels and performance measures, collaboration and the right of the service integrator to act on behalf of the customer.
- Clearly define when a breach of performance becomes a breach of contract. This process is responsible for managing breaches of contract.
- Ensure that contract breaches are addressed consistently and fairly with all service providers.
- Implement practices to support management of multiple contracts, including a contract repository with associated access management.

14.3 Generic process information

14.3.1 Activities

Contract management activities can include:

- Negotiate and agree contracts
- Develop and implement sourcing strategies
- Manage contractual changes
- Verify delivery against contractual requirements
- Address contractual non-compliance

14.3.2 Example roles

Contract management roles can include:

- Contract manager
- Legal advisor

14.3.3 Example metrics

Contract management metrics can include:

- Contract renewals within schedule
- Service provider performance against contracts
- Contract breaches

14.3.4 Example inputs and outputs

Contract management inputs can include:

- New service portfolio entries
- Contract framework
- Contract change notices
- Escalations from supplier management

Contract management outputs can include:

- Service provider addition and removal plans
- Service improvement plans for underperforming service providers
- Contracts
- Warning notices
- Sourcing strategies

15. Process guide: Business relationship management

15.1 Process purpose

The purpose of the business relationship management (BRM) process is to build and maintain strong relationships between service providers and the consumers of their services.

BRM's role is to understand how business processes are supported by a service provider's services and processes. BRM is also responsible for ensuring the right messages are received by the right stakeholders at the right time.

BRM's goal is to create convergence between IT services and business needs, acting as a strategic advisor, rather than a supporting function.

15.2 SIAM considerations

BRM considerations in a SIAM environment include:

- The retained capabilities within the customer organization are normally responsible for BRM with the service consumers
- The service integrator may have its own BRM function that has a relationship with the customer organization's retained capabilities, but this is normally part of the service integrator's commercial activities and does not necessarily form part of the SIAM model
- Service providers may also have BRM functions, which may also be outside the scope of the SIAM model
- A BRM policy should be developed to ensure consistent communication and stakeholder management
- The business areas that consume services must understand that their point of contact for services is via the customer's retained capabilities, and not directly with the service providers

15.3 Generic process information

15.4 Activities

BRM activities can include:

- Developing and maintaining stakeholder engagement plans
- Developing and maintaining communication plans
- Meeting with the service integrator, service providers and customers
- Establishing and maintaining stakeholder forums
- Executing communication plans
- Reviewing customer satisfaction

15.5 Example roles

BRM roles can include:

- Business relationship managers
- Communication managers

- Service owners
- Service managers
- Stakeholders

15.6 *Example metrics*

BRM metrics can include:

- Delivery of communication management plan
- Delivery of communication improvement plans
- Number of improvement initiatives
- Number of satisfaction surveys
- Ratings from satisfaction surveys

15.7 *Example inputs and outputs*

BRM inputs can include:

- Communication standards, including templates, logos and style sheets
- Stakeholder map
- Communication plan
- Customer feedback

BRM outputs can include:

- Communication plan
- Business communications
- Minutes of meetings
- Customer satisfaction reports
- Improvement plans

16. Process guide: Financial management

16.1 Process purpose

The purpose of the financial management process is to oversee the management of the end-to-end financial function and the activities of collating, investigating, analyzing and presenting financial information to the customer.

16.2 SIAM considerations

Financial management considerations in a SIAM environment include:

- Maintaining commercial confidentiality across the ecosystem
- Being able to compare and contrast financial information from different services providers in a meaningful way
- Understanding the cost of a service provided by multiple service providers, including the cost drivers of different components
- Presenting consolidated financial information to the customer in an understandable format
- Maintaining traceability of financial information across the SIAM ecosystem

16.3 Generic process information

16.3.1 Activities

There are six main financial management activities:

- Costing
- Budget planning
- Monitoring of spend against budget
- Producing and maintaining financial reports and outputs
- Conducting financial impact analysis
- Processing invoices

16.3.2 Example roles

Financial management roles can include:

- Chief financial officer
- Management accountant
- Cost accountant
- Accounts assistant

16.3.3 Example metrics

Financial management metrics can include:

- Cost of a service
- Profitability of a service
- Comparison of costs and charges between services and service providers
- Spend against budget

- Accuracy of invoices
- Resolution of invoice discrepancies
- Outputs produced on time

16.3.4 *Example inputs and outputs*

Financial management inputs can include:

- Invoices
- Budget plans
- Contractual pricing models
- Purchase orders
- Service costs

Financial management outputs can include:

- Billing plan
- Reports
- Cost breakdown
- Spend and forecast data
- Financial risk and opportunity information
- Invoice

17. Process guide: Information security management

17.1 Process purpose

The purpose of the information security management (ISM) process is to set and monitor adherence to security policies and processes. It manages the confidentiality, integrity and availability of information, data, IT and people.

Its objective is to protect individuals, technology and organizations from damage caused by system outages, breaches of privacy, malicious attacks and loss or disclosure of protected data and information.

17.2 SIAM considerations

ISM considerations in a SIAM environment include:

- Defining who is accountable for establishing and managing the end-to-end information security process and policies
- Using consistent information security classifications and definitions. For example, what constitutes a security incident?
- Managing and communicating breaches and identified vulnerabilities across the ecosystem
- Defining responsibility for managing the investigation and resolution of security breaches involving multiple parties
- Including security targets within service provider contracts, for example giving the authority to suspend a service provider's service if it is compromising other services
- Being aware of increased security risks when lower-level risks are aggregated across multiple parties

17.3 Generic process information

17.3.1 Activities

ISM activities can include:

- Plan, produce and implement an ISM policy and process
- Enforce the policy and monitor adherence
- Implement a security toolset
- Monitor security activity and take appropriate resolution or improvement actions
- Identify risks derived from aggregation of lower-level risks
- Raise incidents for breaches and failures using the incident management process and service desk
- Evaluate and update the policy, process and tools to ensure protection is maintained
- Plan and deliver training, audits, reviews and tests of the security framework

17.3.2 Example roles

ISM roles can include:

- Senior information risk officer

- Information security manager
- Service desk
- Incident manager

17.3.3 Example metrics

Information security management metrics can include:

- Number of security-related incidents
- Number of security breaches
- Percentage of users complying with security training and other requirements
- Availability and accuracy of security tools and systems
- Accuracy and outcomes of security audits and tests
- Percentage awareness of security principles throughout the organization

17.3.4 Example inputs and outputs

ISM inputs can include:

- Policy requirements
- Regulatory and industry standards
- Previous breach and 'near miss' information
- Planned changes
- Customer and service provider requirements
- Project plans
- Risk logs

ISM outputs can include:

- Security incident records
- Planned improvements
- Remediation activities
- Training needs
- Disciplinary and human resources actions
- Process and policy status reports

18. Process guide: Continual service improvement

18.1 Process purpose

The purpose of the continual service improvement process is to provide a consistent method of quantifying, tracking and managing the delivery of improvement activity across an ecosystem.

Improvement activities can be applied to people, processes, services, technology, and the interfaces and relationships between them.

18.2 SIAM considerations

Continual service improvement considerations in a SIAM environment include:

- A common definition of continual service improvement across all parties in the ecosystem
- The inclusion of continual service improvement on the agenda of governance boards
- Continual service improvement should be the primary focus of the process forum structural elements
- All service providers should be encouraged and incentivized to contribute to continual service improvement activities
- There should be an approach to share lessons to be learned across all parties in the SIAM ecosystem
- There may be a need to establish a central database or register of continual service improvement activities
- The service integrator will be responsible for managing cross-service provider improvements
- There needs to be a mechanism in place to prioritize improvements to the end-to-end services and processes

18.3 Generic process information

18.3.1 Activities

Continual service improvement activities can include:

- Investigation: the improvement is identified and further information obtained
- Baseline: document current metrics
- Identify and quantify the expected or desired improvements and benefits
- Categorize and prioritize the improvement, to define the required level of governance and relative importance
- Approve improvement development and implementation activity
- Stakeholder management and communication planning
- Plan improvement
- Carry out improvement actions
- Review improvement
- Measure, review and quantify benefit
- Close improvement action, including documenting lessons learned

18.3.2 Example roles

Continual service improvement roles can include:

- Improvement initiator
- Improvement sponsor
- Improvement developer/implementer
- Governance board attendees
- Process forum attendees

18.3.3 Example metrics

Continual service improvement metrics can include:

- Number of improvements identified, active and completed
- Cost of improvement activities
- Increased value associated with improvement activities
- Improvements in achievement of service level targets and process performance indicators

18.3.4 Example inputs and outputs

Continual service improvement inputs can include:

- Management information, including service level reports, internal key performance indicator reporting and trend analysis
- Lessons learned reviews
- Audits
- Customer satisfaction reports
- Strategic drivers, including delivery model evaluation, industry benchmarking and governance board outputs

Continual service improvement outputs can include:

- Improvement register
- Management information and recommendations
- Status changes to logged improvements
- Implemented improvements and benefits achieved

19. Process guide: Knowledge management

19.1 Process purpose

The purpose of the knowledge management process is to capture knowledge and make it available to all appropriate people in a controlled and quality-assured manner.

19.2 SIAM considerations

Knowledge management considerations in a SIAM environment include:

- The provision of standardized templates and definitions for knowledge can be useful to assure consistent capture and dissemination
- Service providers should be encouraged to share knowledge with each other
- Responsibilities for creating, reviewing, approving, publishing and maintaining knowledge articles must be clearly defined
- Relevant parties must be able to access knowledge, either from a single knowledge repository or a virtual repository linking all service providers.
- Knowledge should be consistent across the SIAM ecosystem

19.3 Generic process information

19.3.1 Activities

Knowledge management activities can include:

- Knowledge identification, capture and maintenance
- Knowledge transfer
- Data and information management
- Evaluation and improvement

19.3.2 Example roles

Knowledge management roles can include:

- Knowledge creator
- Knowledge manager
- Knowledge editor

19.3.3 Example metrics

Knowledge management metrics can include:

- Number of knowledge users
- Reduction in incident resolution time owing to the use of knowledge items
- Percentage of incidents resolved by referral to knowledge items
- Number of active knowledge articles
- Frequency of updates
- Frequency of access by article

- Accuracy of repository content
- Reduction in time spent on knowledge rediscovery

19.3.4 Example inputs and outputs

Knowledge management inputs can include:

- Documented observations
- External knowledge sources
- Data and process information
- Data repositories
- Release notes
- Procedures manuals
- Training material

Knowledge management outputs can include:

- Knowledge articles
- Reports
- Updated knowledge management system
- Archived data and information
- Updated training materials

20. Process guide: Toolset and information management

20.1 Process purpose

The purpose of the toolset and information management process is to provide toolset(s) to support the other processes, facilitate information sharing and manage data, information and knowledge.

20.2 SIAM considerations

Toolset and information management considerations in a SIAM environment include:

- Defining and managing the use of consistent standards for data, information and knowledge across all service providers
- Creating the toolset strategy for the SIAM model. In SIAM models, there may be a single toolset, or many toolsets
- Creating an enterprise toolset architecture for the SIAM ecosystem
- Selecting an appropriate toolset in line with the strategy and enterprise architecture
- Defining, implementing and maintaining integration between the different parties' toolsets

20.3 Generic process information

20.3.1 Activities

Toolset and information management activities can include:

- Toolset selection
- Toolset implementation
- Toolset management and maintenance
- Data and information standards definition
- Toolset integration

20.3.2 Example roles

Toolset and information management roles can include:

- Toolset architect
- Toolset developer
- Toolset manager
- Data and information architect
- Data and information manager
- Toolset service provider

20.3.3 Example metrics

Toolset and information management metrics can include:

- Toolset availability
- Toolset reliability
- Toolset data quality

20.3.4 *Example inputs and outputs*

Toolset and information management inputs can include:

- Policies and processes for access control
- Configuration data
- Interface schema and designs
- User data
- Data repositories

Toolset and information management outputs can include:

- Toolset
- Performance reports
- Service level reports
- Data and information standards
- Data dictionary
- Data interchange standards
- Information classification

21. Process guide: Project management

21.1 Process purpose

The purpose of the project management process is to provide a structured approach that delivers projects on time, on budget and at the appropriate and agreed level of quality.

21.2 SIAM considerations

Project management in a SIAM environment manages the end-to-end outcomes of projects across multiple service providers.

Considerations in a SIAM environment include:

- The increased complexity of project relationships within a SIAM ecosystem, managing the end-to-end outcomes of projects across multiple service providers
- Accounting for the fact that there is no direct contractual relationship between the service integrator and service providers
- Planning integrated projects involving multiple project teams in multiple service providers
- Obtaining consistency in reporting project status and progress
- Establishment of a collaborative culture to support cross-service provider project management
- Managing risks in integrated projects
- Ensuring effective acceptance into service criteria for project implementations across multiple service providers

21.3 Generic process information

21.3.1 Activities

Project management activities can include:

- Planning
- Adhering to organizational policies and requirements
- Directing actions
- Status reporting
- Risk and issue management
- Delivery of change requests
- Quality management of deliverables
- Managing stakeholders

21.3.2 Example roles

Project management roles can include:

- Project director
- Project manager
- Project management office

21.3.3 *Example metrics*

Project management metrics can include:

- Delivery against plan
- Delivery against quality requirements
- Delivery against budget
- Overdue products
- Customer satisfaction

21.3.4 *Example inputs and outputs*

Project management inputs can include:

- Proposals
- Purchase orders
- Project plans
- Project change requests
- Customer requirements
- Quality criteria

Project management outputs can include:

- Completed projects
- Delivered products
- Plans
- Tasks
- Lessons learned

22. Process guide: Audit and control

22.1 Process purpose

The purpose of the audit and control process is to provide assurance that the services provided to the customer are being delivered in accordance with documented requirements. This can include contracted, legislative, regulatory and security requirements.

22.2 SIAM considerations

Audit and control considerations in a SIAM environment include:

- It is desirable to apply the same governance framework across all parties; however, this may not be possible for certain service providers, for example commodity cloud service providers
- Each organization should own its risks, but the overall accountability for who will ensure that these have been addressed needs to be clearly defined
- The roles of the customer and service integrator in ensuring security assurance and compliance need to be clearly defined
- Requirements need to be in a format that can be understood by auditors and must be clear enough to verify if they are being met
- Audits will need to take place across the whole SIAM ecosystem
- Audits should be conducted on integrated processes involving several service providers, as well as on individual service provider processes
- The rights of the service integrator (or another organization) to carry out audits should be included in contracts with service providers

22.3 Generic process information

22.3.1 Activities

Audit and control activities can include:

- Auditing an organization's processes and systems
- Quality assurance planning
- Auditing services, processes and projects
- Identifying nonconformities against requirements
- Recording, presenting and managing audit findings
- Tracking nonconformities through to closure

22.3.2 Example roles

Audit and control roles can include:

- Quality manager
- Chief security officer
- Auditor
- Service owner
- Process owner

- Project managers

22.3.3 Example metrics

Audit and control metrics can include:

- Compliance against requirements
- Number of nonconformities identified, opened and closed

22.3.4 Example inputs and outputs

Audit and control inputs can include:

- Audit scope
- Requirements
- Policies
- Standards
- Processes
- Data and information records
- Performance reports
- Process metrics

Audit and control outputs consist of audit reports, including:

- Audit scope
- Nonconformities
- Evidence
- Observations
- Risks and issues
- Improvement opportunities

FURTHER READING

IT Governance Publishing (ITGP) is the world's leading publisher for governance and compliance. Our industry-leading pocket guides, books, training resources, and toolkits are written by real-world practitioners and thought leaders. They are used globally by audiences of all levels, from students to C-suite executives.

Our high-quality publications cover all IT governance, risk, and compliance frameworks, and are available in a range of formats. This ensures our customers can access the information they need in the way they need it.

Other resources you may find useful include:

- *Service Integration and Management (SIAM™) Professional Body of Knowledge (BoK), Second edition, www.itgovernancepublishing.co.uk/product/service-integration-and-management-siam-professional-body-of-knowledge-bok-second-edition*
- *ITIL® Foundation Essentials ITIL 4 Edition – The ultimate revision guide, Second edition, www.itgovernancepublishing.co.uk/product/itil-foundation-essentials-itil-4-edition-the-ultimate-revision-guide-second-edition*
- *ITIL® 4 Essentials – Your essential guide for the ITIL 4 Foundation exam and beyond, Second edition, www.itgovernancepublishing.co.uk/product/itil-4-essentials-your-essential-guide-for-the-itil-4-foundation-exam-and-beyond-second-edition*

For more information on ITGP and branded publishing services, and to view our full list of publications, visit *www.itgovernancepublishing.co.uk*.

To receive regular updates from ITGP, including information on new publications in your area(s) of interest, sign up for our newsletter at *www.itgovernancepublishing.co.uk/topic/newsletter*.

Branded publishing

Through our branded publishing service, you can customize ITGP publications with your organization's branding.

Find out more at *www.itgovernancepublishing.co.uk/topic/branded-publishing-services*.

Related services

ITGP is part of GRC International Group, which offers a comprehensive range of complementary products and services to help organizations meet their objectives.

For a full range of resources visit *www.itgovernance.co.uk*.

Training services

The IT Governance training program is built on our extensive practical experience designing and implementing management systems based on ISO standards, best practice, and regulations.

Our courses help attendees develop practical skills and comply with contractual and regulatory requirements. They also support career development via recognized qualifications.

Learn more about our training courses and view the full course catalog at *www.itgovernance.co.uk/training*.

Professional services and consultancy

We are a leading global consultancy of IT governance, risk management, and compliance solutions. We advise organizations around the world on their most critical issues, and present cost-saving and risk-reducing solutions based on international best practice and frameworks.

We offer a wide range of delivery methods to suit all budgets, timescales, and preferred project approaches.

Find out how our consultancy services can help your organization at *www.itgovernance.co.uk/consulting*.

Industry news

Want to stay up to date with the latest developments and resources in the IT governance and compliance market? Subscribe to our Weekly Round Up newsletter and we will send you mobile-friendly emails with fresh news and features about your preferred areas of interest, as well as unmissable offers and free resources to help you successfully start your projects. *www.itgovernance.co.uk/weekly-round-up*.

Lightning Source UK Ltd.
Milton Keynes UK
UKHW051158180721
387295UK00005B/2